COMPLETE
Thai
COOKING

PARRAGON

STEP-BY-STEP

COMPLETE

Thai

COOKING

CAROL BOWEN

CARA HOBDAY

SUE ASHWORTH

First published in Great Britain in 1995 by
Parragon
Unit 13–17
Avonbridge Trading Estate
Atlantic Road
Avonmouth
Bristol BS11 9QD
Copyright © Parragon 1995

Reprinted in 1997

ISBN 0-7525-0136-4

Printed in Italy

Acknowledgements:
Art Direction: Ron Samuels
Editors: Beverly LeBlanc, Diana Vowles
Page Design: Pedro & Frances Prá-Lopez /Kingfisher Design
Jacket Design: Somewhere Creative
Photography: Sue Atkinson, Iain Bagwell, Martin Brigdale
Home Economists: Sue Ashworth, Jill Eggleton, Cara Hobday
Styling: Sue Atkinson, Rachel Jukes, Helen Trent
Step-by-Step Photography Section 1: Karl Adamson
Step-by-Step Home Economist Section 1: Joanna Craig

Photographs on pages 12, 24, 34, 58, 72, 86, 100, 112, 128, 144,
158, 174, 186, 202 and 214 reproduced by permission of ZEFA
Picture Library (UK) Ltd.

Material contained in this book has previously appeared in
Thai Cooking, Vegetarian Thai Cooking and *Thai Side Dishes.*

Note:
*Cup measurements in this book are for American cups. Tablespoons are
assumed to be 15ml. Unless otherwise stated, milk is assumed to be full-
fat, eggs are standard size 2 and pepper is freshly ground black pepper.*

Contents

COMPLETE
Thai
COOKING

In recent years Thai cuisine has become
increasingly popular in the West, its fresh,
zingy flavours being perfectly suited to the
current trend for light, healthy eating and an
eagerness to explore all kinds of food from
the world's cooking pot.

Not only is Thai food tasty and nutritionally
excellent, it is also easy and quick to prepare.
Most of the characteristic ingredients are
now readily available and substitutes can be
used for those that are harder to find. Those
who like it hot can step up the chillies, while
more tender palates will find plenty of dishes
to please them. There's something for
everyone in Thai cooking – so arm yourself
with a sharp knife, a wok or frying pan and a
rice pot, and *bon appetit!*

1

THAI COOKING

CHAPTER ONE

Starters

From the spicy exuberance of a hot and sour duck salad to the more subtle flavours of a chicken or beef satay, the importance of the starter-style dish has long been recognized and celebrated in Thai households. Unlike Western cuisine, however, it is more likely to be served before a meal with drinks, as a snack between meals, as party or celebration food, or as a dish that is served just before and then with the main course.

Typically several dishes of this type are served at once in the age-old tradition of enticing and tempting the appetite or teasing the palate. In the pages that follow you will find a selection of such tempting entrées from baby fish cakes with a tasty cucumber garnish; tiny skewered chicken or beef kebabs called satay that are served with a flavoursome peanut sauce; a colourful array of crisp vegetable crudités served with a Thai shrimp dipping sauce; and mouth-watering hot and sour or sweet and sour crisp salad mixtures.

Fortunately for the cook these are dishes that can be prepared well ahead of time or can be assembled and cooked very quickly. Consider too some of the main-course recipes in bite-sized portions – Barbecued Chicken Legs (see page 38) and Duck with Ginger and Lime (see page 49) double up beautifully as starter or main course fare.

Opposite: *The fishing fleet returns at sunset to Kata Beach, Phuket.*

RED CURRY FISHCAKES

Just the thing to entice the tastebuds, Thai fishcakes make a tasty starter and good introduction to a Thai-style meal. Almost any kind of fish fillets or seafood can be used.

STEP 2

MAKES ABOUT 24 (TO SERVE 4–6)

1 kg/2 lb fish fillets or prepared seafood, such as cod, haddock, prawns (shrimp), crab meat or lobster
1 egg, beaten
2 tbsp chopped fresh coriander (cilantro)
1 quantity Red Curry Paste (see page 36)
1 bunch spring onions (scallions), chopped finely
vegetable oil for deep-frying
chilli flowers, to garnish

CUCUMBER SALAD:
1 large cucumber, peeled and grated
2 shallots, grated
2 red chillies, deseeded and chopped very finely
2 tbsp fish sauce
2 tbsp dried powdered shrimps
1¹/₂–2 tbsp lime juice

1 Place the fish in a blender or food processor with the egg, coriander (cilantro) and curry paste and purée until smooth and well blended.

2 Turn the mixture into a bowl, add the spring onions (scallions) and mix well to combine.

STEP 3

3 Taking 2 tablespoons of the fish mixture at a time, shape into balls, then flatten them slightly with your fingers to make fishcakes.

4 Heat the oil in a wok or frying pan (skillet) until hot, add a few of the fishcakes and deep-fry for a few minutes until brown and cooked through. Remove with a slotted spoon and drain on paper towels. Keep warm while cooking the remaining fishcakes.

5 Meanwhile, to make the cucumber salad, mix the cucumber with the shallots, chillies, fish sauce, dried shrimps and lime juice.

6 Serve the salad immediately, with the warm fishcakes.

STEP 4

CHILLIES

When handling chillies be very careful not to touch your face or eyes: chilli juice is a powerful irritant, and can be very painful on the skin. Always wash your hands after preparing chillies.

STEP 5

CRUDITES WITH SHRIMP SAUCE

This is a classic Thai starter – fruit and vegetable crudités served with a spicy, garlicky shrimp sauce. It is served at every meal, and each family has its own favourite recipe.

STEP 1

SERVES 6

about 750 g/ 1½ lb prepared raw fruit and vegetables, such as broccoli, cauliflower, apple, pineapple, cucumber, celery, (bell) peppers and mushrooms

SAUCE:
60 g/ 2 oz dried shrimps
1 cm/½ in cube shrimp paste
3 garlic cloves, crushed
4 red chillies, deseeded and chopped
6 stems fresh coriander (cilantro), chopped coarsely
juice of 2 limes
fish sauce, to taste
brown sugar, to taste

1 Soak the dried shrimps in warm water for 10 minutes.

2 To make the sauce, place the shrimp paste, drained shrimps, garlic, chillies and coriander (cilantro) in a food processor or blender and process until well chopped but not smooth.

3 Turn the sauce mixture into a bowl and add the lime juice, mixing well.

4 Add fish sauce and brown sugar to taste to the sauce, mixing to blend

well. Cover the bowl tightly and chill the sauce in the refrigerator for at least 12 hours or overnight.

5 To serve, arrange the fruit and vegetables attractively on a large serving plate. Place the prepared sauce in the centre for dipping.

STEP 2

STEP 3

ALTERNATIVE

Hard-boiled quail's eggs are often added to this traditional fruit and vegetable platter and certainly would be offered on a special occasion.

STEP 4

STEP 2

STEP 3

STEP 4

STEP 5

SWEET & SOUR TOFU (BEAN CURD) SALAD

Tofu (bean curd) is a delicious, healthy alternative to meat. Mixed with a variety of crisp stir-fried vegetables, then tossed in a piquant sweet and sour dressing, it makes an ideal light meal or starter.

SERVES 4–6

2 tbsp vegetable oil
1 tbsp sesame oil
1 garlic clove, crushed
500 g/1 lb tofu (bean curd), cubed
1 onion, sliced
1 carrot, cut into julienne strips
1 stick celery, sliced
2 small red (bell) peppers, cored, deseeded and sliced
250 g/8 oz mangetout (snow peas), trimmed and halved
125 g/4 oz broccoli, trimmed and divided into florets
125g/4 oz thin green beans, halved
2 tbsp oyster sauce
1 tbsp tamarind concentrate
1 tbsp fish sauce
1 tbsp tomato purée (paste)
1 tbsp light soy sauce
1 tbsp chilli sauce
2 tbsp sugar
1 tbsp white vinegar
pinch ground star anise
1 tsp cornflour (cornstarch)
300 ml/$^1/_2$ pint/1$^1/_4$ cups water

1 Heat the vegetable oil in a large, heavy-based frying pan (skillet) or wok until hot. Add the crushed garlic and cook for a few seconds.

2 Add the tofu (bean curd) in batches and stir-fry over a gentle heat until golden on all sides. Remove with a slotted spoon and keep warm.

3 Add the onion, carrot, celery, red (bell) pepper, mangetout (snow peas), broccoli and green beans to the pan and stir-fry for about 2–3 minutes or until tender-crisp.

4 Add the oyster sauce, tamarind concentrate, fish sauce, tomato purée (paste), soy sauce, chilli sauce, sugar, vinegar and star anise, mixing well to blend. Stir-fry for a further 2 minutes.

5 Mix the cornflour (cornstarch) with the water and add to the pan with the fried tofu. Stir-fry gently until the sauce boils and thickens slightly.

6 Serve the salad immediately, on warm plates.

STEP 1

STEP 2

STEP 3

STEP 5

CHICKEN OR BEEF SATAY

A favourite Thai dish that can be made with chicken or beef and served with a spicy peanut sauce.

SERVES 4–6

4 boneless, skinned chicken breasts or
  750 g/1¹/₂ lb rump steak, trimmed

MARINADE:
1 small onion, chopped finely
1 garlic clove, crushed
2.5 cm/1 inch piece ginger root, peeled and
  grated
2 tbsp dark soy sauce
2 tsp chilli powder
1 tsp ground coriander
2 tsp dark brown sugar
1 tbsp lemon or lime juice
1 tbsp vegetable oil

SAUCE:
300 ml/¹/₂ pint/1¹/₄ cups coconut milk
4 tbsp crunchy peanut butter
1 tbsp fish sauce
1 tsp lemon or lime juice
salt and pepper

1 Trim any fat from the chicken or beef, then cut into thin strips about 7 cm/3 inches long.

2 To make the marinade, place all the ingredients in a shallow dish and mix well. Add the chicken or beef strips and turn in the marinade until well coated. Cover and leave to marinate for 2 hours or stand overnight in the refrigerator.

3 Remove the meat from the marinade and thread the pieces, concertina style, on to bamboo or thin wooden skewers.

4 Grill (broil) the chicken and beef satays for 8–10 minutes, turning and brushing occasionally with the marinade until cooked through.

5 Meanwhile, to make the sauce, mix the coconut milk with the peanut butter, fish sauce and lemon juice in a pan. Bring to the boil and cook for 3 minutes. Season to taste and serve with the cooked satays.

SATAY STICKS

Fine bamboo or wooden skewers are traditionally used to cook satays. Soak in cold water for at least 1 hour to prevent them burning and scorching during cooking.

HOT & SOUR DUCK SALAD

This is a lovely tangy salad, drizzled with a lime juice and Thai fish sauce dressing. It makes a splendid starter or light main course dish.

STEP 1

SERVES 4

2 heads crisp salad lettuce, washed and separated into leaves
2 shallots, sliced thinly
4 spring onions (scallions), chopped
1 celery stick, sliced finely into julienne strips
5 cm/2 inch piece cucumber, cut into julienne strips
125 g/4 oz bean-sprouts
200 g/7 oz canned water chestnuts, drained and sliced
4 duck breast fillets, roasted and sliced (see page 49)
orange slices, to serve

DRESSING:
3 tbsp fish sauce
1½ tbsp lime juice
2 garlic cloves, crushed
1 red chilli pepper, deseeded and chopped very finely
1 green chilli pepper, deseeded and chopped very finely
1 tsp palm or demerara sugar

1 Mix the lettuce leaves with the shallots, spring onions (scallions), celery, cucumber, bean-sprouts and water chestnuts. Place the mixture on a large serving platter.

2 Arrange the duck breast slices on top of the salad in an attractive overlapping pattern.

3 To make the dressing, put the fish sauce, lime juice, garlic, chillies and sugar into a small pan. Heat gently, stirring constantly. Taste and adjust the piquancy if liked by adding more lime juice, or add more fish sauce to reduce the sharpness.

4 Drizzle the warm salad dressing over the duck salad and serve immediately.

STEP 2

STEP 3

JULIENNE STRIPS

To cut vegetables into julienne strips, first slice thinly into even-sized slices. Stack the slices on top of each other, then cut with a sharp knife into very thin shreds.

STEP 4

CHAPTER TWO

Fish & Seafood

It is not surprising that fish and seafood feature prominently on the
typical Thai menu, as so much of the country is surrounded
by water. Whole fresh fish are often simply charcoal-grilled,
steamed, fried or baked. Many are baked in banana leaves to keep
the flesh moist and succulent. Seafood is often skewered and
barbecued or sizzled in a wok with rice, chillies, nuts and other
finely sliced or diced vegetables to make a quick and tasty one-pot
meal. Both fish and seafood are also given the pungent-flavoured
treatment in a whole host of curries from mild and mellow to
fiery and fierce. Fruit such as pineapple, paw-paw (papaya) and
mango may also be added to give a flavour
and texture contrast.

Whatever the fish the golden rule is to choose seafood that is
absolutely at the peak of freshness. Look for whole fish that has
bright eyes, red gills, firm flesh, shiny scales and a fresh sea-like
odour. Never settle for second best! Likewise choose seafood
that is still tightly locked and closed in its shell.
Discard those that are already open.

Opposite: *Fishing boats
moored on Chon Khram beach,
Koh Samui Island. The seas
around Thailand teem with fish
of every kind.*

STEP 1

STEP 2

STEP 3

FRIED RICE & PRAWNS (SHRIMP)

When you've got one eye on the clock and a meal to make this is the one! Made in a trice, yet simply stunning to look at, its taste belies its simplicity.

SERVES 4

60 g/2 oz/¼ cup butter
3 tbsp vegetable oil
500 g/1 lb/3 cups cooked basmati rice
6 spring onions (scallions), sliced finely
125 g/4 oz mangetout (snow peas), halved
1 carrot, cut into fine julienne strips
125 g/4 oz canned water chestnuts, drained
  and sliced
1 small crisp lettuce, shredded
350 g/12 oz peeled tiger prawns (shrimp)
1 large red chilli, deseeded and sliced
  diagonally
3 egg yolks
4 tsp sesame oil
salt and pepper

1 Heat the butter and the oil in a large, heavy-based frying pan (skillet) or wok. Add the cooked rice and stir-fry for 2 minutes.

2 Add the spring onions (scallions), mangetout (snow peas), carrot, water chestnuts and salt and pepper to taste, mixing well. Stir-fry over a medium heat for a further 2 minutes.

3 Add the shredded lettuce, prawns (shrimp) and chilli and stir-fry for a further 2 minutes.

4 Beat the egg yolks with the sesame oil and stir into the pan, coating the rice and vegetable mixture. Cook for about 2 minutes to set the egg mixture.

5 Serve the rice and prawns (shrimp) at once on warmed plates.

FRIED RICE

For perfect fried rice, it is best to cook the rice ahead of time and allow it to cool completely before adding to the hot oil. In that way the rice grains will remain separate, and the rice will not become lumpy or heavy.

SIZZLED CHILLI PRAWNS (SHRIMP)

*Another Thai classic – large prawns (shrimp) marinated in a chilli
mixture and then stir-fried with cashews. Serve with a fluffy rice
and braised vegetables.*

STEP 1

STEP 2

STEP 3

STEP 4

SERVES 4

5 tbsp soy sauce
5 tbsp dry sherry
3 dried red chillies, deseeded and chopped
2 garlic cloves, crushed
2 tsp grated ginger root
5 tbsp water
625 g/ 1¼ lb shelled tiger prawns (shrimp)
1 large bunch spring onions (scallions),
    chopped
90 g/ 3 oz/²/₃ cup salted cashew nuts
3 tbsp vegetable oil
2 tsp cornflour (cornstarch)

1 Mix the soy sauce with the sherry,
chillies, garlic, ginger and water in
a large bowl.

2 Add the prawns (shrimp), spring
onions (scallions) and cashews and
mix well. Cover tightly and leave to
marinate for at least 2 hours, stirring
occasionally.

3 Heat the oil in a large, heavy-based
frying pan (skillet) or wok. Drain
the prawns (shrimp), spring onions
(scallions) and cashews from the
marinade with a slotted spoon and add to
the pan, reserving the marinade. Stir-fry
over a high heat for 1–2 minutes.

4 Mix the reserved marinade with the
cornflour (cornstarch), add to the
pan and stir-fry for about 30 seconds
until the marinade forms a slightly
thickened shiny glaze over the prawn
(shrimp) mixture.

5 Serve the prawns (shrimp)
immediately, with rice.

VARIATION

For an attractive presentation serve this
dish on mixed wild rice and basmati or
other long-grain rice. Start cooking the
wild rice in boiling water. After 10
minutes, add the basmati rice or other rice
and continue boiling until all grains are
tender. Drain well and adjust the
seasoning.

STEP 1

STEP 2

STEP 2

STEP 3

PINEAPPLE & FISH CURRY

This is a fiery hot Thai curry dish all the better for serving with refreshing (and cooling) fresh pineapple pieces.

SERVES 4

2 pineapples
7 cm/ 3 in piece galangal, sliced
2 stalks lemon grass, bruised then chopped
5 sprigs fresh basil
500 g/ 1 lb firm white fish fillets, cubed
    (monkfish, halibut or cod, for example)
125 g/ 4 oz peeled prawns (shrimp)
2 tbsp vegetable oil
2 tbsp Red Curry Paste (see page 36)
125 ml/ 4 fl oz/ $^1/_2$ cup thick coconut milk or
    cream
2 tbsp fish sauce
2 tsp palm or demarara sugar
2–3 red chillies, deseeded and cut into thin
    julienne strips
about 6 kaffir lime leaves, torn into pieces
coriander (cilantro) sprigs, to garnish

1 Cut the pineapples in half lengthways. Remove the flesh, reserving the shells if using (see right). Remove the core from the pineapple flesh, then dice into bite-sized pieces.

2 Place the galangal in a large shallow pan with the lemon grass and basil. Add the fish cubes and just enough water to cover. Bring to the boil, reduce the heat and simmer for about 2 minutes. Add the prawns (shrimp) and

cook for a further 1 minute or until the fish is just cooked. Remove from the flavoured stock with a slotted spoon and keep warm.

3 Heat the oil in a heavy-based frying pan (skillet) or wok. Add the curry paste and cook for 1 minute. Stir in the coconut milk or cream, fish sauce, brown sugar, chillies and lime leaves.

4 Add the pineapple and cook until just heated through. Add the cooked fish and mix gently to combine.

5 Spoon into the reserved pineapple shells, if liked, and serve immediately, garnished with sprigs of coriander (cilantro).

VARIATION

This dish could be served on plates, but for a stunning presentation on a special occasion, serve in the hollowed-out shells of the pineapple.

WRAPPED FISH WITH GINGER BUTTER

This is fish cooked in a healthy, palate-tingling way. Whole mackerel or trout are stuffed with herbs, wrapped in foil or, more authentically, banana leaves, baked and then drizzled with a fresh ginger butter.

STEP 1

SERVES 4
OVEN: 190°C/375°F/GAS MARK 5

4 × 250 g/8 oz whole trout or mackerel, gutted
4 tbsp chopped fresh coriander (cilantro)
5 garlic cloves, crushed
2 tsp grated lemon or lime rind
2 tsp vegetable oil
banana leaves for wrapping (optional)
90 g/3 oz/6 tbsp butter
1 tbsp grated ginger root
1 tbsp light soy sauce
salt and pepper
coriander (cilantro) sprigs and lemon or lime wedges, to garnish

1 Wash and dry the fish. Mix the coriander (cilantro) with the garlic, lemon or lime rind and salt and pepper to taste. Spoon into the fish cavities.

2 Brush the fish with a little oil, season well and place each fish on a double thickness sheet of baking parchment or foil and wrap up well to enclose. Alternatively, wrap in banana leaves (see right).

3 Place on a baking sheet (cookie sheet) and bake in the preheated

STEP 2

oven for about 25 minutes or until the flesh will flake easily.

4 Meanwhile, melt the butter in a small pan. Add the grated ginger and stir until well mixed, then stir in the soy sauce.

5 To serve, unwrap the fish parcels, drizzle over the ginger butter and garnish with coriander (cilantro) and lemon or lime wedges.

STEP 2

BANANA LEAVES

For a really authentic touch, wrap the fish in banana leaves, which can be ordered from specialist oriental supermarkets. They are not edible, but impart a delicate flavour to the fish.

STEP 3

CHAPTER THREE

Meat & Poultry

Unlike many other oriental nationalities, the Thais are not restricted by religion over what they can eat, so pork, beef and lamb appear with poultry on the menu. However, since quantities can be scarce by Western standards, the Thais invent imaginative dishes that cunningly stretch limited supplies to the full.

Hence you will find wonderful meats stretched with noodles, chicken stir-fried with an array of vegetables, beef extended with glistening shredded bok choy cabbage, and meats simmered and stretched with vegetables in a coconut milk and chilli paste sauce.

You'll also find some old favourites with the Thai inspirational twist – chicken roasted with the addition of lemon grass, kaffir lime leaves, ginger, coriander (cilantro) and garlic; and fried beef steak, the steak cut into strips and stir-fried with coloured (bell) peppers, spring onions (scallions), celery, mushrooms, onions and crunchy cashew nuts, all the better for serving with a mound of fluffy rice and a few braised vegetables.

Opposite: Every imaginable kind of foodstuff is for sale in this floating market at Damnoen Saduak, south of Bangkok.

STEP 2

STEP 3

STEP 4

STEP 5

RED CHICKEN CURRY

The chicken is cooked with a curry paste using red chillies (see below).
It is a fiery hot sauce – for a milder version, reduce the number of
chillies used.

SERVES 6

4 tbsp vegetable oil
2 garlic cloves, crushed
400 ml/14 fl oz/1¾ cups coconut milk
6 chicken breast fillets, skinned and cut into
  bite-sized pieces
125 ml/4 fl oz/½ cup chicken stock
2 tbsp fish sauce
kaffir lime leaves, sliced red chillies and
  chopped coriander (cilantro), to garnish

RED CURRY PASTE:
8 dried red chillies, deseeded and chopped
2.5 cm/1 in galangal or ginger root, peeled
  and sliced
3 stalks lemon grass, chopped
1 garlic clove, peeled
2 tsp shrimp paste
1 kaffir lime leaf, chopped
1 tsp ground coriander
¾ tsp ground cumin
1 tbsp chopped fresh coriander (cilantro)
1 tsp salt and black pepper

1 To make the curry paste, place all the ingredients in a food processor or blender and process until smooth.

2 Heat the oil in a large, heavy-based frying pan (skillet) or wok. Add the garlic and cook for 1 minute or until it turns golden, stirring occasionally.

3 Stir in the curry paste and cook for 10–15 seconds, then gradually add the coconut milk, stirring constantly (don't worry if the mixture starts to look curdled at this stage).

4 Add the chicken pieces and turn in the sauce mixture to coat. Cook gently for about 3–5 minutes or until almost tender.

5 Stir in the chicken stock and fish sauce, mixing well, then cook for a further 2 minutes.

6 Transfer to a warmed serving dish and garnish with lime leaves, sliced red chillies and chopped coriander (cilantro). Serve with rice.

CURRY PASTE

There are two basic curry pastes used in Thai cuisine – red and green, depending upon whether they are made from red or green chilli peppers. The basic paste can be made and stored in a lidded jar in the refrigerator for up to two weeks.

STEP 2

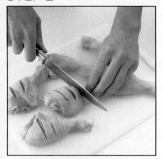

STEP 3

STEP 4

STEP 5

BARBECUED CHICKEN LEGS

Just the thing to put on the barbecue – chicken legs, coated with a spicy, curry-like butter, then grilled until crispy and golden. Serve with a crisp green seasonal salad and rice.

SERVES 6

12 chicken drumsticks

SPICED BUTTER:
175 g/6 oz/³/₄ cup butter
2 garlic cloves, crushed
1 tsp grated ginger root
2 tsp ground turmeric
4 tsp chilli powder
2 tbsp lime juice
3 tbsp mango chutney

1 Prepare a barbecue with medium coals or preheat a conventional grill (broiler) to medium.

2 To make the spiced butter mixture, beat the butter with the garlic, ginger, turmeric, chilli powder, lime juice and chutney until it is blended well.

3 Using a sharp knife, slash each chicken leg to the bone 3–4 times.

4 Cook the drumsticks over the barbecue for 12–15 minutes or until almost cooked. Alternatively, grill (broil) the chicken for about 10–12 minutes until almost cooked, turning halfway through.

5 Spread the chicken legs liberally with the butter mixture and continue to cook for a further 5–6 minutes, turning and basting frequently with the butter until golden and crisp.

6 Serve hot or cold with a crisp green salad and rice.

VARIATION

This spicy butter mixture would be equally effective on grilled (broiled) chicken or turkey breast fillets. Skin before coating with the mixture.

STEP 2

STEP 3

STEP 5

STEP 5

ROAST BABY CHICKENS

Poussins, stuffed with lemon grass and lime leaves, coated with a spicy Thai paste, then roasted until crisp and golden, make a wonderful, aromatic dish for a special occasion.

SERVES 4
OVEN: 200°C/400°F/GAS MARK 6

4 small poussins, weighing 350–500 g/
 12 oz–1 lb each
about 6 tbsp coconut milk, to brush
coriander (cilantro) leaves and lime wedges,
 to garnish
a mixture of wild rice and basmati rice,
 to serve

MARINADE:
4 garlic cloves, peeled
2 fresh coriander (cilantro) roots
1 tbsp light soy sauce
salt and pepper

STUFFING:
4 blades lemon grass
4 kaffir lime leaves
4 slices ginger root

1 Wash the chickens and dry on paper towels.

2 Place all the ingredients for the marinade in a small blender and purée until smooth, or grind in a pestle and mortar. Season to taste with salt and pepper. Rub this marinade mixture into the skin of the chickens, using the back of a spoon to spread it evenly over the skins.

3 Place a blade of lemon grass, a lime leaf and a piece of ginger in the cavity of each chicken.

4 Place the chickens in a roasting tin (pan) and brush lightly with the coconut milk. Roast for 30 minutes in the preheated oven.

5 Remove from the oven, brush again with coconut milk, return to the oven and cook for a further 15–25 minutes, until golden and cooked through, depending upon the size of the chickens. The chickens are cooked when the juices from the thigh run clear and are not tinged at all with pink.

6 Serve with the pan juices poured over. Garnish with coriander (cilantro) leaves and lime wedges.

GREEN CHILLI CHICKEN

The green chilli paste gives a hot and spicy flavour to the chicken, which takes on a vibrant green colour.

SERVES 4

5 tbsp vegetable oil
500 g/ 1 lb boneless chicken breasts, sliced into thin strips
50 ml/ 2 fl oz/¼ cup coconut milk
3 tbsp brown sugar
3 tsp fish sauce
3 tbsp sliced red and green chillies, deseeded
4–6 tbsp chopped fresh basil
3 tbsp thick coconut milk or cream
finely chopped fresh chillies,deseeded, lemon grass and lemon slices, to garnish

GREEN CURRY PASTE:
2 tsp ground ginger
2 tsp ground coriander
2 tsp caraway seeds,
2 tsp grated nutmeg
2 tsp shrimp paste
2 tsp salt
2 tsp black pepper
pinch ground cloves
1 stalk lemon grass, chopped finely
2 tbsp chopped coriander (cilantro)
2 garlic cloves, peeled
2 onions, peeled
grated rind and juice of 2 limes
4 fresh green chillies, about 5 cm/ 2 inches long, deseeded

1 To make the curry paste, place all the ingredients and 2 tablespoons of the oil in a food processor or blender and process to a smooth paste.

2 Heat the remaining oil in a heavy-based frying pan (skillet) or wok. Add the curry paste and cook for about 30 seconds.

STEP 2

3 Add the chicken strips to the wok and stir-fry over a high heat for 2–3 minutes.

STEP 3

4 Add the coconut milk, brown sugar, fish sauce and chillies. Cook for 5 minutes, stirring frequently.

5 Remove from the heat, add the basil and toss well to mix.

STEP 4

6 Transfer the chicken to a warmed serving dish. To serve, spoon on a little of the thick coconut milk or cream and garnish with chopped chillies, lemon grass and lemon slices. Serve with steamed or boiled rice.

STEP 5

STEP 1

STEP 2

STEP 3

STEP 4

PEANUT SESAME CHICKEN

In this quickly prepared dish chicken strips are stir-fried with vegetables. Sesame and peanuts give extra crunch and flavour and the fruit juice glaze gives a lovely shiny coating to the sauce.

SERVES 4

2 tbsp vegetable oil
2 tbsp sesame oil
500g/ 1 lb boneless, skinned chicken breasts, sliced into strips
250 g/ 8 oz broccoli, divided into small florets
250 g/ 8 oz baby corn, halved if large
1 small red (bell) pepper, cored, deseeded and sliced
2 tbsp soy sauce
250 ml/ 8 fl oz/ 1 cup orange juice
2 tsp cornflour (cornstarch)
2 tbsp toasted sesame seeds
60 g/ 2 oz/$^1/_3$ cup roasted, shelled, unsalted peanuts

1 Heat the oils in a large, heavy-based frying pan (skillet) or wok. Add the chicken strips and stir-fry for 4–5 minutes until browned.

2 Add the broccoli, corn and red (bell) pepper and stir-fry for a further 1–2 minutes.

3 Meanwhile, mix the soy sauce with the orange juice and cornflour (cornstarch). Stir into the chicken and vegetable mixture, stirring constantly until the sauce has slightly thickened and a glaze develops.

4 Stir in the sesame seeds and peanuts, mixing well. Heat for a further 3–4 minutes, then serve at once, with rice or noodles.

PEANUTS

Make sure you use the unsalted variety of peanuts or the dish will be too salty, as the soy sauce adds saltiness.

CHICKEN & NOODLE ONE-POT

Flavoursome chicken and vegetables cooked with Chinese egg noodles in a coconut sauce. Serve in deep soup bowls.

STEP 1

SERVES 4

1 tbsp sunflower oil
1 onion, sliced
1 garlic clove, crushed
2.5 cm/1 inch ginger root, peeled and grated
1 bunch spring onions (scallions),
    diagonally sliced
500 g/1 lb chicken breast fillet, skinned and
    cut into bite-sized pieces
2 tbsp mild curry paste
475 ml/16 fl oz/2 cups coconut milk
300 ml/$\frac{1}{2}$ pint/1$\frac{1}{4}$ cups chicken stock
250 g/8 oz Chinese egg noodles
2 tsp lime juice
salt and pepper
basil sprigs, to garnish

1 Heat the oil in a large, heavy-based frying pan (skillet) or wok. Add the onion, garlic, ginger and spring onions (scallions) and stir-fry for 2 minutes until softened.

2 Add the chicken pieces and curry paste and stir-fry until the vegetables and chicken are golden brown, about 4 minutes.

3 Stir in the coconut milk, stock and salt and pepper to taste, mixing until well blended.

4 Bring to the boil, break the noodles into large pieces, if necessary, add to the pan, cover and simmer for about 6–8 minutes until the noodles are just tender, stirring occasionally.

5 Add the lime juice, taste and adjust the seasoning, if necessary, then serve at once in deep soup bowls.

STEP 2

STEP 3

COOK'S TIP

If you enjoy the hot flavours of Thai cooking then substitute the mild curry paste in the above recipe with Thai hot curry paste (found in most supermarkets) but reduce the quantity to 1 tablespoon.

STEP 4

DUCK WITH GINGER & LIME

Just the thing for a lazy summer day – roasted duck breasts sliced and served with a dressing made of ginger root, lime juice, sesame oil and fish sauce. Serve on a bed of assorted fresh salad leaves.

STEP 1

SERVES 6
OVEN: 200°C/400°F/GAS MARK 6

3 boneless Barbary duck breasts, about
    250 g/8 oz each
salt

DRESSING:
125 ml/4 fl oz/½ cup olive oil
2 tsp sesame oil
2 tbsp lime juice
grated rind and juice of 1 orange
2 tsp fish sauce
1 tbsp grated ginger root
1 garlic clove, crushed
2 tsp light soy sauce
3 spring onions (scallions), chopped finely
1 tsp sugar
about 250 g/8 oz assorted salad leaves
orange slices, to garnish (optional)

1 Wash the duck breasts, dry on paper towels, then cut in half. Prick the skin all over with a fork and season well with salt. Place the duck pieces, skin-side down, on a wire rack or trivet over a roasting tin (pan). Cook the duck in the preheated oven for 10 minutes, then turn over and cook for a further 12–15 minutes or until the duck is cooked, but still pink in the centre and the skin is crisp.

2 To make the dressing, beat the oils with the lime juice, orange rind and juice, fish sauce, ginger, garlic, soy sauce, spring onions (scallions) and sugar until well blended.

3 Remove the duck from the oven, allow to cool, then cut into thick slices. Add a little of the dressing to moisten and coat the duck.

4 To serve, arrange assorted salad leaves on a serving dish. Top with the sliced duck breasts and drizzle with the remaining salad dressing.

5 Garnish with orange twists, if using, then serve at once.

STEP 1

STEP 2

STEP 3

COOK'S TIP

If an extra crisp skin is preferred on the duck then quickly fry the duck breasts, skin-side down, in a non-stick pan (without any additional oil) for a few minutes until golden. Cook in the oven as above, but reduce the cooking time by about 3 minutes.

BEEF & BOK CHOY

A colourful selection of vegetables stir-fried with tender strips of steak.

STEP 1

STEP 2

STEP 3

STEP 3

SERVES 4

1 large head bok choy, about 250–275 g/
   8–9 oz, torn into large pieces
2 tbsp vegetable oil
2 garlic cloves, crushed
500 g/1 lb rump or fillet steak, cut into thin
   strips
150 g/5 oz mangetout (snow peas),
   trimmed
150 g/5 oz baby corn
6 spring onions (scallions), chopped
2 red (bell) peppers, cored, deseeded and
   sliced thinly
2 tbsp oyster sauce
1 tbsp fish sauce
1 tbsp sugar

1 Steam the bok choy leaves over boiling water until just tender. Keep warm.

2 Heat the oil in a large, heavy-based frying pan (skillet) or wok. Add the garlic and steak strips and stir-fry for 1–2 minutes until just browned.

3 Add the mangetout (snow peas), baby corn, spring onions (scallions), red (bell) pepper, oyster sauce, fish sauce and sugar to the pan, mixing well. Stir-fry for a further 2–3

minutes until the vegetables are just tender, but still crisp.

4 Arrange the bok choy leaves in the base of a heated serving dish and spoon the beef and vegetable mixture into the centre.

5 Serve the stir-fry immediately, with rice or noodles.

VARIATION

Bok choy is one of the most important ingredients in this dish. If unavailable, use Chinese leaves, kai choy (mustard leaves) or pak choy.

GREEN BEEF CURRY

This is a quickly made curry prepared with strips of beef steak, cubed aubergine (eggplant) and onion in a cream sauce flavoured with green curry paste. Serve with fluffy rice and a salad.

STEP 1

SERVES 4

1 aubergine (eggplant), peeled and cubed
2 onions, cut into thin wedges
2 tbsp vegetable oil
1 quantity Green Curry Paste (see page 43)
500 g/1 lb beef fillet, cut into thin strips
475 ml/16 fl oz/2 cups thick coconut milk
  or cream
2 tbsp fish sauce
1 tbsp brown sugar
1 red chilli, deseeded and chopped very finely
1 green chilli, deseeded and chopped finely
2.5 cm/1 in piece ginger root, chopped finely
4 kaffir lime leaves, torn into pieces
chopped fresh basil, to garnish

1 Blanch the aubergine (eggplant) cubes and onion wedges in boiling water for about 2 minutes, to soften. Drain thoroughly.

2 Heat the oil in a large, heavy-based frying pan (skillet) or wok. Add the curry paste and cook for 1 minute.

3 Add the beef strips and stir-fry over a high heat for about 1 minute to brown on all sides.

4 Add the coconut milk or cream, fish sauce and sugar to the pan and

STEP 2

bring the mixture to the boil, stirring constantly.

5 Add the aubergine (eggplant) and onion, chillies, ginger and lime leaves. Cook for a further 2 minutes.

6 Sprinkle with chopped basil to serve. Accompany with rice.

STEP 3

THICK COCONUT MILK

Coconut milk is sold in cans, or you can make your own. Pour 300 ml/½ pint/1¼ cups boiling water over 250 g/8 oz shredded coconut and simmer over low heat for 30 minutes. Strain the milk into a bowl through a piece of muslin (cheesecloth). Gather the ends of the muslin (cheesecloth) together and squeeze tightly to extract as much liquid as possible.

STEP 4

STEP 1

STEP 2

STEP 4

STEP 5

PEPPERED BEEF CASHEW

A simple but stunning dish of tender strips of beef mixed with crunchy cashew nuts, coated in a hot sauce. Serve with rice noodles.

SERVES 4

1 tbsp groundnut or sunflower oil
1 tbsp sesame oil
1 onion, sliced
1 garlic clove, crushed
1 tbsp grated ginger root
500 g/ 1 lb fillet or rump steak, cut into thin
    strips
2 tsp palm or demerara sugar
2 tbsp light soy sauce
1 small yellow (bell) pepper, cored, deseeded
    and sliced
1 red (bell) pepper, cored, deseeded and sliced
4 spring onions (scallions), chopped
2 celery sticks, chopped
4 large open-cap mushrooms, sliced
4 tbsp roasted cashew nuts
3 tbsp stock or white wine

1 Heat the oils in a large, heavy-based frying pan (skillet) or wok. Add the onion, garlic and ginger and stir-fry for about 2 minutes until softened and lightly coloured.

2 Add the steak strips and stir-fry for a further 2–3 minutes until the meat has browned.

3 Add the sugar and soy sauce, mixing well.

4 Add the (bell) peppers, spring onions (scallions), celery, mushrooms and cashews, mixing well.

5 Add the stock or wine and stir-fry for 2–3 minutes until the beef is cooked through and the vegetables are tender-crisp.

6 Serve the stir-fry immediately with rice noodles.

PALM SUGAR

Palm sugar is a thick brown sugar with a slightly caramel taste. It is sold in cakes, or in small containers. If not available, use soft dark brown or demerara sugar.

GARLIC PORK & SHRIMPS

This is a wonderful one-pot dish of stir-fried pork fillet (tenderloin) with shrimps and noodles that is made in minutes. Serve straight from the pan.

STEP 1

SERVES 4

250 g/8 oz Chinese egg noodles
3 tbsp vegetable oil
2 garlic cloves, crushed
350 g/12 oz pork fillet (tenderloin), cut into strips
4 tbsp/⅓ cup dried shrimps, or 125 g/4 oz peeled prawns (shrimp)
1 bunch spring onions (scallions), chopped finely
90 g/3 oz/¾ cup chopped roasted and shelled unsalted peanuts
3 tbsp fish sauce
1½ tsp palm or demerara sugar
1–2 small red chillies, deseeded and chopped finely (to taste)
3 tbsp lime juice
3 tbsp chopped fresh coriander (cilantro)
chives, to garnish

1 Place the noodles in a large pan of boiling water, then immediately remove from the heat. Cover and leave to stand for 6 minutes, stirring once halfway through the time. At the end of 6 minutes the noodles will be perfectly cooked. Alternatively, follow the packet instructions. Drain the noodles thoroughly and keep warm.

2 Heat the oil in a large, heavy-based frying pan (skillet) or wok. Add the garlic and pork and stir-fry for 2–3 minutes until the pork strips are browned.

3 Add the dried shrimps or shelled prawns (shrimp), spring onions (scallions), peanuts, fish sauce, sugar, chillies to taste and lime juice. Stir-fry for a further 1 minute.

4 Add the cooked noodles and coriander (cilantro) and stir-fry for about 1 minutes until heated through. Serve the stir-fry immediately, garnished with chives. If you prefer, the dish can be prepared with rice as an accompaniment rather than adding in the noodles.

STEP 2

STEP 3

FISH SAUCE

Fish sauce is made from pressed, salted fish and is widely available in supermarkets and oriental stores. It is very salty, so no extra salt should be added.

STEP 4

CHAPTER FOUR

Accompaniments

Good Thai food is a happy marriage of many different dishes that contrast in flavour, colour and texture. Rice may well be the staple food, but freshly cooked plain long-grain rice is only one way of serving this basic. In countless other dishes it is baked, steamed, stir-fried and boiled with an almost infinite spectrum of vegetables, herbs, spices and flavourings to entice and delight.

Noodles too have a major role to play when snacks come to the fore. Many noodles, fried with just a few extra ingredients, make superb light meals to enjoy in their own right. No self-respecting Thai would do without the bowl of mid-day noodles!

The Thais also employ clever ways with their rich supply of vegetables such as shallots, garlic, baby corn, cabbage, green beans, broccoli, (bell) peppers and mushrooms. Sliced and diced they are used in imaginative stir-fries; cubed and sliced they are braised in aromatic broths and sauces; and finely shredded they make exciting, palate-tingling salads with exotic dressings using limes, fish sauce, ginger, soy sauce and sesame oil.

Opposite: *A basket stall in the floating market in Bangkok.*

THAI SALAD

This is a typical Thai-style salad made by mixing fruit and vegetables with the sharp, sweet and fishy flavours of the dressing.

STEP 1

SERVES 4–6

250 g / 8 oz white cabbage, shredded finely
2 tomatoes, skinned, deseeded and chopped
250 g / 8 oz cooked green beans, halved if large
125 g / 4 oz peeled prawns (shrimp)
1 paw-paw (papaya), peeled, deseeded and chopped
1–2 fresh red chillies, deseeded and sliced very finely
60 g / 2 oz / scant ¹/₃ cup roasted salted peanuts, crushed
handful lettuce or baby spinach leaves, shredded or torn into small pieces
coriander (cilantro) sprigs, to garnish

DRESSING:
4 tbsp lime juice
2 tbsp fish sauce
sugar, to taste
pepper

2 Line the rim of a large serving plate with the lettuce or spinach and pile the salad mixture into the centre.

STEP 2

3 To make the dressing, beat the lime juice with the fish sauce and add sugar and pepper to taste. Drizzle over the salad.

4 Scatter the top with the remaining paw-paw (papaya), chillies and crushed peanuts. Garnish with coriander (cilantro) leaves and serve at once.

STEP 3

1 Mix the cabbage with the tomatoes, green beans, prawns (shrimp), three-quarters of the paw-paw (papaya) and half the chillies in a bowl. Stir in two-thirds of the crushed peanuts and mix together well.

SKINNING TOMATOES

To skin tomatoes, make a cross at the base with a very sharp knife, then immerse in a bowl of boiling water for a few minutes. Remove with a slotted spoon and peel off the skin.

STEP 4

THAI FRAGRANT COCONUT RICE

This is the finest rice to serve with Thai-style food. Basmati rice is cooked with creamed coconut, lemon grass, fresh ginger root and spices to make a wonderfully aromatic, fluffy rice.

STEP 1

SERVES 4–6

2.5 cm/1 in piece ginger root, peeled and
   sliced
2 cloves
1 piece lemon grass, bruised and halved
2 tsp grated nutmeg
1 cinnamon stick
1 bay leaf
2 small thin strips lime rind
1 tsp salt
30 g/1 oz creamed coconut, chopped
600 ml/1 pint/2½ cups water
350 g/12 oz/1¾ cups basmati rice
ground pepper

1 Place the ginger, cloves, lemon grass, nutmeg, cinnamon stick, bay leaf, lime rind, salt, creamed coconut and water in a large, heavy-based pan and bring slowly to the boil.

2 Add the rice, stir well, then cover and simmer, over a very gentle heat for about 15 minutes or until all the liquid has been absorbed and the rice is tender but still has a bite to it.

3 Remove from the heat, add pepper to taste, then fluff up the rice with a fork. Remove the large pieces of spices before serving.

LEMON GRASS

When using a whole stalk of lemon grass (rather than chopped lemon grass), beat it well to bruise it so the flavour is fully released. Grated lemon rind or a pared piece of lemon rind can be used instead.

COOKING RICE

An alternative method of cooking the rice – the absorption method – leaves you free to concentrate on other dishes. Add the rice to the pan as in step 1, then bring back to the boil. Stir well, then cover tightly and turn off the heat. Leave for 20–25 minutes before removing the lid – the rice will be perfectly cooked.

STEP 2

STEP 3

SESAME HOT NOODLES

Plain egg noodles are all the better when tossed in a dressing made with nutty sesame oil, soy sauce, peanut butter, coriander (cilantro), lime juice, chilli and sesame seeds. Serve hot as a main meal accompaniment.

STEP 1

SERVES 6

500 g/ 1 lb Chinese egg noodles
3 tbsp sunflower oil
2 tbsp sesame oil
1 garlic clove, crushed
1 tbsp smooth peanut butter
1 small green chilli, deseeded and chopped
    very finely
3 tbsp toasted sesame seeds
4 tbsp light soy sauce
1–2 tbsp lime juice
salt and pepper
4 tbsp chopped fresh coriander (cilantro)

1 Place the noodles in a large pan of boiling water, then immediately remove from the heat. Cover and leave to stand for 6 minutes, stirring once halfway through the time. At the end of 6 minutes the noodles will be perfectly cooked. Otherwise follow packet instructions.

2 Meanwhile, to make the dressing, mix the oils with the garlic and peanut butter until smooth.

3 Add the chilli, sesame seeds, soy sauce and lime juice, according to taste and mix well. Season with salt and pepper.

4 Drain the noodles thoroughly then place in a heated serving bowl. Add the dressing and coriander (cilantro) and toss well to mix. Serve immediately.

STEP 2

STEP 3

COOKING NOODLES

If you are cooking noodles ahead of time, toss the cooked, drained noodles in 2 teaspoons sesame oil, then turn into a bowl. Cover and keep warm.

STEP 4

STEP 2

STEP 3

STEP 4

STEP 4

THAI FRIED RICE

The Thais often serve their rice fried, but not just plain and simple – they give theirs an extra punch and bit of a zip with hot red chillies, spring onions (scallions) and fish sauce.

SERVES 4

250 g/8 oz/1 cup basmati rice
3 tbsp sunflower oil
1 hot red chilli, deseeded and chopped finely
2 tsp fish sauce
3 spring onions (scallions), chopped
1 large egg, beaten
1 tbsp chopped parsley or coriander
  (cilantro)
1 tbsp soy sauce
1 tsp sugar
salt and pepper

1 Cook the rice in boiling salted water for about 10 minutes until tender. Drain, rinse with boiling water and drain again. Spread out on a large plate or baking sheet (cookie sheet) to dry.

2 Heat the oil in a large, heavy-based frying pan (skillet) or wok until hot. Add the chilli, fish sauce and spring onions (scallions) and stir-fry for 1–2 minutes.

3 Add the beaten egg and stir-fry quickly so that the egg scrambles into small fluffy pieces.

4 Fork through the rice to separate the grains, then add to the pan and stir-fry for about 1 minute to mix and heat through.

5 Sprinkle a little of the chopped parsley over the rice. Mix the soy sauce with the sugar and remaining chopped parsley and stir into the rice mixture, tossing well to mix. Serve immediately.

FRIED RICE

For perfect fried rice it is important that the rice is thoroughly dry and cold before it is added to the pan, otherwise it may become lumpy and soggy.

THAI BRAISED VEGETABLES

This colourful selection of braised vegetables makes a splendid accompaniment to a main dish.

STEP 1

SERVES 4–6

3 tbsp sunflower oil
1 garlic clove, crushed
1 Chinese cabbage, shredded thickly
2 onions, cut into wedges
250 g / 8 oz broccoli florets
2 large carrots, cut into thin julienne strips
12 baby corn, halved if large
60 g / 2 oz mangetout (snow peas),
  halved
90 g / 3 oz Chinese or oyster mushrooms,
  sliced
1 tbsp grated ginger root
175 ml / 6 fl oz / ³⁄₄ cup vegetable stock
2 tbsp light soy sauce
1 tbsp cornflour (cornstarch)
salt and pepper
¹⁄₂ tsp sugar

1 Heat the oil in a large, heavy-based frying pan (skillet) or wok. Add the garlic, cabbage, onions, broccoli, carrots, baby corn, mangetout (snow peas), mushrooms and ginger and stir-fry for 2 minutes.

2 Add the stock, cover and cook for a further 2–3 minutes.

3 Blend the soy sauce with the cornflour (cornstarch) and salt and pepper to taste.

STEP 2

4 Remove the braised vegetables from the pan with a slotted spoon and keep warm. Add the soy sauce mixture to the pan juices, mixing well. Bring to the boil, stirring constantly, until the mixture thickens slightly. Stir in the sugar.

5 Return the vegetables to the pan and toss in the slightly thickened sauce. Cook gently to just heat through then serve immediately.

STEP 3

VARIATION

This dish also makes an ideal vegetarian main meal. Double the quantities, to serve 4–6, and serve with noodles or Thai Fried Rice (see page 66).

STEP 5

SOUPS & STARTERS

•

RICE & NOODLES

•

MAIN COURSE DISHES

•

VEGETABLES

•

BUFFET DISHES

2

VEGETARIAN THAI COOKING

CHAPTER FIVE

Soups & Starters

Food and hospitality are an important part of daily life in the countries of South-East Asia. In Thailand, the traditional way to share the pleasures of eating together is to sit down with your family and friends to a meal that is served as one course of many different dishes. Usually a fried dish, a steamed or stewed dish and a curry are arranged around a communal bowl of steaming, fluffy, fragrant rice, and a bowl of soup is served alongside.

Although there is usually no first course in traditional Thai meals, one may often find that smaller dishes are served before the main course in restaurants in Thailand that cater for foreigners and tourists, or in Thai restaurants in other countries where a light starter is usual. It is pleasant to have an appetizer as a prelude to the meal to follow, and there are many dishes in the Thai cuisine that make excellent appetizers.

Opposite: *An extraordinary rock formation graces the shores of Phuket in southern Thailand.*

STEP 1

STEP 2

STEP 3

STEP 3

HOT & SOUR SOUP

A very traditional staple of the Thai national diet, this soup is sold on street corners, at food bars and by mobile vendors all over the country.

SERVES 4

1 tbsp sunflower oil
250 g/8 oz smoked tofu (bean curd),
  sliced
90 g/3 oz/1 cup shiitake mushrooms,
  sliced
2 tbsp chopped fresh coriander (cilantro)
125 g/4 oz/2 cups watercress
1 red chilli, sliced finely, to garnish

STOCK:
1 tbsp tamarind pulp
2 dried red chillies, chopped
2 kaffir lime leaves, torn in half
2.5 cm/1 inch piece ginger root, chopped
5 cm/2 inch piece galangal, chopped
1 stalk lemon grass, chopped
1 onion, quartered
1 litre/1 3/4 pints/4 cups cold water

1 Put all the ingredients for the stock into a saucepan and bring to the boil. Simmer for 5 minutes. Remove from the heat and strain, reserving the stock.

2 Heat the oil in a wok or large, heavy frying pan (skillet) and cook the tofu (bean curd) over a high heat for about 2 minutes, stirring constantly. Add the strained stock.

3 Add the mushrooms and coriander (cilantro), and boil for 3 minutes. Add the watercress and boil for 1 minute.

4 Serve immediately, garnished with red chilli slices.

MUSHROOMS

You might like to try a mixture of different types of mushroom. Oyster, button and straw mushrooms are all suitable.

STEP 1

STEP 3

STEP 4

STEP 5

NOODLE, MUSHROOM & GINGER SOUP

Thai soups are very quickly and easily put together, and are cooked so that each ingredient can still be tasted, even after it has been combined with several others.

SERVES 4

15 g/¹/₂ oz/¹/₄ cup dried Chinese mushrooms
  or 125 g/4 oz/1¹/₃ cups field or chestnut
  (crimini) mushrooms
1 litre/1³/₄ pints/4 cups hot vegetable stock
125 g/4 oz thread egg noodles
2 tsp sunflower oil
3 garlic cloves, crushed
2.5 cm/1 inch piece ginger root, shredded
  finely
¹/₂ tsp mushroom ketchup
1 tsp light soy sauce
125 g/4 oz/2 cups bean-sprouts
 coriander (cilantro) leaves to garnish

1 Soak the dried Chinese mushrooms, if using, for at least 30 minutes in 300 ml/¹/₂ pint/1¹/₄ cups of the hot vegetable stock. Remove the stalks and discard, then slice the mushrooms. Reserve the stock.

2 Cook the noodles for 2–3 minutes in boiling water. Drain and rinse. Set them aside.

3 Heat the oil over a high heat in a wok or large, heavy frying pan (skillet). Add the garlic and ginger, stir and add the mushrooms. Stir over a high heat for 2 minutes.

4 Add the remaining vegetable stock with the reserved stock and bring to the boil. Add the mushroom ketchup and soy sauce.

5 Stir in the bean-sprouts. Cook until tender and serve immediately over the noodles, garnished with coriander (cilantro) leaves.

CHINESE MUSHROOMS

Dried Chinese mushrooms are widely available from all oriental stores and markets and from many specialist food shops and delicatessens. They are quite inexpensive and will keep for an extended period in a sealed jar.

FILLED CUCUMBER CUPS

There are two types of Thai cooking: the elaborate Royal cooking, and the peasant style of cooking. This dish is from the Royal cuisine, where care is taken over presentation, and the flavours are subtle.

STEP 1

SERVES 6

1 cucumber
4 spring onions (scallions), chopped finely
4 tbsp lime juice
2 small red chillies, deseeded and chopped finely
3 tsp sugar
150 g/ 5 oz/ 1¼ cups ground roasted peanuts
¼ tsp salt
3 shallots, sliced finely and deep-fried, to garnish

5 Divide the filling between the 6 cucumber cups and arrange on a serving plate. Garnish with the deep-fried shallots.

STEP 2

1 To make the cucumber cups, cut the ends off the cucumber, and divide it into 3 equal lengths. Mark a line around the centre of each one as a guide.

2 Make a zigzag cut all the way around the centre of each section, always pointing the knife towards the centre of the cucumber. Pull apart the 2 halves.

3 Scoop out the centre of each cup with a melon baller or teaspoon.

STEP 4

4 Put the remaining ingredients, except for the shallots, in a bowl and mix well to combine.

> ### CHERRY TOMATOES
>
> Cherry tomatoes can also be hollowed out very simply with a melon baller and filled with this mixture. The two look very pretty arranged together on a serving dish.

STEP 5

STEP 1

STEP 2

STEP 3

STEP 5

RICE CUBES WITH DIPPING SAUCE

Plain rice cubes are a good foil to any piquant dipping sauce, and they are often served with satay, to complement the dipping sauce.

SERVES 4–6

300 g/10 oz/1½ cups Thai jasmine rice
1.25 litres/2¼ pints/5 cups water

CORIANDER (CILANTRO) DIPPING
  SAUCE:
1 garlic clove
2 tsp salt
1 tbsp black peppercorns
60 g/2 oz/1 cup washed coriander
  (cilantro), including roots and stem
3 tbsp lemon juice
180 ml/6 fl oz/¾ cup coconut milk
2 tbsp peanut butter
2 spring onions (scallions), chopped roughly
1 red chilli, deseeded and sliced

1 Grease and line a 20 × 10 × 2.5 cm/8 × 4 × 1 inch tin.

2 To make the sauce, put the garlic, salt, peppercorns, coriander (cilantro) and lemon juice into a pestle and mortar or blender. Grind finely.

3 Add the coconut milk, peanut butter, spring onions (scallions) and chilli. Grind finely. Transfer to a saucepan and bring to the boil. Leave to cool. This sauce will keep for 3–5 days in a refrigerator.

4 To cook the rice, do not rinse. Bring the water to the boil and add the rice. Stir and return to a medium boil. Cook, uncovered, for 14–16 minutes until very soft. Drain thoroughly.

5 Put 125 g/4 oz/⅔ cup of the cooked rice in a blender and purée, or grind to a paste in a pestle and mortar. Stir into the remaining cooked rice and spoon into the lined tin (pan). Level the surface and cover with clingfilm (plastic wrap). Compress the rice by using either a similar-sized tin (pan) which will fit into the filled tin (pan), or a small piece of board, and weigh this down with cans. Chill for at least 8 hours or preferably overnight.

6 Invert the tin (pan) on to a board. Cut the rice into cubes with a wet knife. Serve with the coriander (cilantro) dipping sauce.

RICE

This recipe would work equally well with basmati rice, but avoid using any rice labelled 'easy cook' or 'par-boiled' as you will have disappointing results.

STEP 1

STEP 2

STEP 3

STEP 5

FRIED TOFU (BEAN CURD) WITH PEANUT SAUCE.

This is another very sociable dish if you put it in the centre of the table where people can help themselves with cocktail sticks.

SERVES 4

*500 g/1 lb tofu (bean curd), marinated or
    plain
2 tbsp rice vinegar
2 tbsp sugar
1 tsp salt
3 tbsp smooth peanut butter
½ tsp chilli flakes
3 tbsp barbecue sauce
1 litre/1¾ pints/4 cups sunflower oil
2 tbsp sesame oil*

*BATTER:
4 tbsp plain (all-purpose) flour
2 eggs, beaten
4 tbsp milk
½ tsp baking powder
½ tsp chilli powder*

1 Cut the tofu (bean curd) into
2.5 cm/1 inch triangles. Set aside.

2 Combine the vinegar, sugar and
salt in a saucepan. Bring to the boil
and then simmer for 2 minutes. Remove
from the heat and add the peanut butter,
chilli flakes and barbecue sauce.

3 To make the batter, sift the flour
into a bowl, make a well in the
centre and add the eggs. Draw in the
flour, adding the milk slowly. Stir in the
baking powder and chilli powder.

4 Heat both the oils in a deep-fryer or
large saucepan until a light haze
appears on top.

5 Dip the tofu (bean curd) triangles
into the batter and deep-fry until
golden brown. Drain on paper towels.

6 Serve with the peanut sauce.

FRYING TOFU

You may find it easier to pick up the tofu
(bean curd) triangles on a fork or skewer
in order to coat them in batter before
placing them in the hot oil.

STEP 1

STEP 2

STEP 3

STEP 4

AUBERGINE (EGGPLANT) DIPPING SAUCE PLATTER

Dipping platters are a very sociable dish, bringing the whole table together. Serve this substantial dip with vegetables as an appetizer.

SERVES 4

1 aubergine (eggplant), peeled and cut into
  2.5 cm/ 1 inch cubes
3 tbsp sesame seeds, roasted in a dry pan
  over a low heat
1 tsp sesame oil
grated rind and juice of ½ lime
1 small shallot, diced
½ tsp salt
1 tsp sugar
1 red chilli, deseeded and sliced
125 g/4 oz/ 1¼ cups broccoli florets
2 carrots, cut into matchsticks
125 g/4 oz/8 baby corn, cut in half
  lengthways
2 celery sticks, cut into matchsticks
1 baby red cabbage, cut into 8 wedges, the
  leaves of each wedge held together by the
  core

1 Cook the diced aubergine (eggplant) in boiling water for 7–8 minutes.

2 Meanwhile, grind the sesame seeds with the oil in a food processor or pestle and mortar.

3 Add the aubergine (eggplant), lime rind and juice, shallot, salt, sugar and chilli in that order to the sesame.

4 Process, or chop and mash by hand, until smooth, Check for seasoning before spooning into a bowl. Serve surrounded by the broccoli, carrots, baby corn, celery and red cabbage.

SALTING
AUBERGINES
(EGGPLANTS)

Unlike in Western kitchens, Thais never salt aubergines (eggplants) as theirs are so fresh and tender.

CHAPTER SIX

Rice & Noodles

The Thai signal that the meal is ready is *Kin khao* – literally translated this means 'eat rice'. Thai jasmine rice is the central part of the Thai diet, and every meal is based around it. Thais are in the habit of eating rice, and will eat at one sitting about twice as much as the average Westerner would, so naturally they are exacting about the quality of their rice, the taste, fragrance and whiteness of it, and will pay for these points in a superior rice.

Nearly all modern Thai women possess at least two rice cookers each and would be lost if asked to cook rice in a Western kitchen. Unlike our rice cookers, the Asian version is a sophisticated piece of equipment. But for the Western cook without a fancy rice cooker the absorption method is best, though there are two important things to remember: do not stir too much while the rice is cooking, as this will release the starch in the rice, and make it stick together; and if you plan to reuse the rice, cool it down quickly by spreading it out on a tray and refrigerating it. When reheating ensure that it is hot through, and reheat it only once.

Noodles are eaten at any time of the day or night in Thailand, as a fast food prepared by numerous roadside vendors, who will whip up, before your very eyes, a tasty and spicy noodle dish to see you through to the next food stop, which will not be very far away.

Opposite: *A moat temple in Chiang Mai presents a peaceful scene.*

METHOD 1: STEP 1

METHOD 1: STEP 2

METHOD 2: STEP 2

METHOD 2: STEP 3

THAI JASMINE RICE

Every Thai meal has as its centrepiece a big bowl of steaming, fluffy Thai jasmine rice. The method used for cooking rice in Thailand is the absorption method, but also given below is the open pan method, as this is the one most familiar to Western cooks. Salt should not be added.

SERVES 3–4

1: OPEN PAN METHOD
250 g/8 oz/generous 1 cup Thai jasmine
*   rice*
1 litre/1 ³⁄₄ pints/4 cups water

1 Rinse the rice in a sieve (strainer) under cold running water and leave to drain.

2 Bring the water to the boil. Add the rice, stir and return to a medium boil. Cook, uncovered, for 8–10 minutes.

3 Drain and fork through lightly before serving.

2: ABSORPTION METHOD
250 g/8 oz/generous 1 cup Thai jasmine
*   rice*
450 ml/³⁄₄ pint/scant 2 cups water

1 Rinse the rice in a sieve (strainer) under cold running water.

2 Put the rice and water into a saucepan and bring to the boil. Stir once and then cover the pan tightly. Lower the heat as much as possible. Cook for 10 minutes. Leave to rest for 5 minutes.

3 Fork through lightly and serve immediately.

STEP 1

STEP 2

STEP 4

STEP 4

GREEN RICE

A deliciously different way to serve plain rice for a special occasion or to liven up a simple meal.

SERVES 4

2 tbsp olive oil
500 g/ 1 lb/ 2¼ cups basmati or Thai
    jasmine rice, soaked for 1 hour, washed
    and drained
750 ml/ 1¼ pints/ 3 cups coconut milk
1 tsp salt
1 bay leaf
2 tbsp chopped fresh coriander (cilantro)
2 tbsp chopped fresh mint
2 green chillies, deseeded and chopped
    finely

1 Heat the oil in a saucepan, add the rice and stir until it becomes translucent.

2 Add the coconut milk, salt and bay leaf. Bring to the boil and cook until all the liquid is absorbed.

3 Lower the heat as much as possible, cover the saucepan tightly and cook for 10 minutes.

4 Remove the bay leaf and stir in the coriander (cilantro), mint and green chillies. Fork through the rice gently and serve.

GARNISHES

The contrasting colours of this dish make it particularly attractive, and it can be made to look even more interesting with a carefully chosen garnish. Two segments of fresh lime complement the coriander (cilantro) perfectly. Alternatively, you could simply use some small sprigs of whole fresh coriander (cilantro) leaves.

COOKING IN A MICROWAVE

To save time, or to make some room on your stove, step 3 can be done in a microwave. Transfer the rice to a microwave container, cover tightly and cook on High for 4–5 minutes. Remove the bay leaf, and stir in the herbs and chillies. Fork through the rice gently and serve.

STEP 1

STEP 2

STEP 3

STEP 3

CHATUCHAK FRIED RICE

An excellent way to use up leftover rice! Pop it in the freezer as soon as it is cool. It will be ready to use at any time, and the freezing seems to separate the grains beautifully. This dish should be reheated only once.

SERVES 4

1 tbsp sunflower oil
3 shallots, chopped finely
2 garlic cloves, crushed
1 red chilli, deseeded and chopped finely
2.5 cm/1 inch piece ginger root, shredded
  finely
½ green (bell) pepper, sliced finely
150 g/5 oz/2–3 baby aubergines
  (eggplants), quartered
90 g/3 oz sugar snap peas or mangetout
  (snow peas), trimmed and blanched
90 g/3 oz/6 baby corn, halved lengthways
  and blanched
1 tomato, cut into 8 pieces
90 g/3 oz/1½ cups bean-sprouts
500 g/1 lb/3 cups cooked Thai jasmine rice
  (see page 88)
2 tbsp tomato ketchup
2 tbsp light soy sauce

TO GARNISH:
coriander (cilantro) leaves
lime wedges

1 Heat the oil in a wok or large, heavy frying pan (skillet) over a high heat. Add the shallots, garlic, chilli and ginger. Stir until the shallots have softened.

2 Add the green (bell) pepper and baby aubergines (eggplants) and stir. Add the sugar snap peas or mangetout (snow peas), baby corn, tomato and bean-sprouts. Stir together for 3 minutes.

3 Add the rice, and lift and stir with 2 spoons for 4–5 minutes until no more steam is released. Stir in the tomato ketchup and soy sauce.

4 Serve immediately, garnished with coriander (cilantro) leaves and lime wedges to squeeze over.

VARIATION

Almost any vegetable, such as celery, aubergine (eggplant), water chestnuts, bamboo shoots, carrots, beans, cauliflower or broccoli can be used. Harder vegetables may need blanching first, to ensure all the vegetables will cook in the same amount of time.

STEP 1

THAI-STYLE STIR-FRIED NOODLES

This dish is considered the Thai national dish, as it is made and eaten everywhere – a one-dish fast food for eating on the move.

SERVES 4

250 g/8 oz dried rice noodles
2 red chillies, deseeded and chopped finely
2 shallots, chopped finely
2 tbsp sugar
2 tbsp tamarind water
1 tbsp lime juice
2 tbsp light soy sauce
black pepper
1 tbsp sunflower oil
1 tsp sesame oil
175 g/6 oz/³/₄ cup smoked tofu (bean curd), diced
2 tbsp chopped roasted peanuts

1 Cook the rice noodles as directed on the pack, or soak them in boiling water for 5 minutes.

2 Grind together the chillies, shallots, sugar, tamarind water, lime juice, light soy sauce and black pepper.

3 Heat both the oils together in a wok or large, heavy frying pan (skillet) over a high heat. Add the tofu (bean curd) and stir for 1 minute.

4 Add the chilli mixture, bring to the boil, and stir for about 2 minutes until thickened.

4 Drain the rice noodles and add them to the chilli mixture. Use 2 spoons to lift and stir them until they are no longer steaming. Serve immediately, garnished with the peanuts.

STEP 2

STEP 3

ONE-DISH MEAL

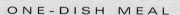

This is a quick one-dish meal that is very useful if you are catering for a single vegetarian in the family.

STEP 4

STEP 1

STEP 2

STEP 3

STEP 4

CRISPY DEEP-FRIED NOODLES

This is the staple dish on every Thai restaurant menu by which the establishment will be judged. It does require a certain amount of care and attention to get the crispy noodles properly cooked.

SERVES 4

175 g/6 oz Chinese egg noodles
600 ml/1 pint/2½ cups sunflower oil for
   deep-frying
2 tsp grated lemon rind
1 tbsp light soy sauce
1 tbsp rice vinegar
1 tbsp lemon juice
1½ tbsp sugar
250 g/8 oz/1 cup marinated tofu (bean
   curd), diced
2 garlic cloves, crushed
1 red chilli, sliced finely
1 red (bell) pepper, cored, deseeded and diced
4 eggs, beaten
red chilli, sliced, to garnish

1 Blanch the egg noodles briefly in hot water, to which a little of the oil has been added. Drain and spread out to dry for at least 30 minutes. Cut into threads about 7 cm/3 inches long.

2 Combine the lemon rind, light soy sauce, rice vinegar, lemon juice and sugar in a small bowl.

3 Heat the oil in a wok or large, heavy frying pan (skillet), and test the temperature with a few strands of noodles. They should swell to many times their size, but if they do not, wait until the oil is hot enough; otherwise they will be tough and stringy, not puffy and light. Cook them in batches. As soon as they turn a pale gold colour, scoop them out and drain on plenty of paper towels. Leave to cool.

4 Reserve 2 tablespoons of the oil and drain off the rest. Heat the 2 tablespoons of oil in the wok or frying pan (skillet). Cook the tofu (bean curd) quickly over a high heat to seal. Add the garlic, chilli and diced (bell) pepper. Stir for 1–2 minutes. Add the vinegar mixture to the pan, stir and add the eggs, stirring until they are set.

5 Serve with the crispy fried noodles, garnished with sliced red chilli.

PERFECT NOODLES

For best results with this dish, the oil must be hot enough and the noodles must be drained on paper towels immediately.

STEP 1

STEP 2

STEP 3

STEP 4

FRIED NOODLES WITH BEAN-SPROUTS, CHIVES & CHILLI

This is a simple idea to jazz up noodles which accompany main course dishes in Thailand.

SERVES 4

500 g/1 lb medium egg noodles
60 g/2 oz/1 cup bean-sprouts
15 g/¹/₂ oz chives
3 tbsp sunflower oil
1 garlic clove, crushed
4 green chillies, deseeded, sliced and soaked
  in 2 tbsp rice vinegar
salt

1 To cook the noodles, soak in boiling water for 10 minutes. Drain and set aside.

2 Soak the bean-sprouts in cold water while you cut the chives into 2.5cm/1 inch pieces. Set a few chives aside for garnish. Drain the bean-sprouts thoroughly.

3 Heat the oil in a wok or large, heavy frying pan (skillet). Add the crushed garlic and stir; then add the chillies and stir until fragrant, about 1 minute.

4 Add the bean-sprouts, stir and then add the noodles. Stir in some salt and the chives. Using 2 spoons, lift and stir the noodles for 1 minute.

5 Garnish the finished dish with the reserved chives, and serve immediately.

CHILLIES

Soaking a chilli in rice vinegar has the effect of distributing the hot chilli flavour throughout the dish. To reduce the heat, you can slice the chilli more thickly before soaking, or soak it once, discard the vinegar, then soak again in a second batch of vinegar before adding the vinegar and chilli to the dish.

HERBS

A variety of fresh herbs can be stirred through rice and noodles to make them a little special. Coriander (cilantro) and mint are a very successful combination.

CHAPTER SEVEN

Main Course Dishes

Thai cookery is based on a very different set of rules, methods and techniques from those by which we cook in the West. Thai cooks often have to work with only what is available; this, combined with the various simple cooking methods of stir-frying, steaming and deep-frying, means that the cuisine is wide open to interpretation. One dish can have four different tastes in four different regions and the variety of dishes is as infinite as the number of cooks.

People's tastes and kitchens vary widely in other countries too, so do not be afraid to adapt and experiment with these recipes. For instance, you could try substituting another firm vegetable in the Aubergine (Eggplant) & Mushroom Satay with Peanut Sauce or extending the Massaman Curried Rice with extra vegetables. Adapt the recipes to your personal preference and to the fresh produce available – and do not forget the Thai spirit of *Sanuk* – fun!

STEP 1

STEP 2

STEP 3

STEP 4

RED CURRY WITH CASHEWS

This is a wonderfully quick dish to prepare. The paste can be bought ready-prepared and is very satisfactory, but it has a delicious aroma when homemade. It will keep for up to 3 weeks in the refrigerator.

SERVES 4

3 tbsp Red Curry Paste (see below)
250 ml/8 fl oz/1 cup coconut milk
1 kaffir lime leaf, mid-rib removed
¼ tsp light soy sauce
60 g/2 oz/4 baby corn, halved lengthways
125 g/4 oz/1¼ cups broccoli florets
125 g/4 oz green beans, cut into 5 cm/
    2 inch pieces
30 g/1 oz/¼ cup cashew nuts
15 fresh basil leaves
1 tbsp chopped fresh coriander (cilantro)
1 tbsp chopped roast peanuts, to garnish

RED CURRY PASTE:
7 fresh red chillies, halved, deseeded and
    blanched (use dried if fresh are not
    available)
2 tsp cumin seeds
2 tsp coriander seeds
2.5 cm/1 inch piece galangal, peeled and
    chopped
½ stalk lemon grass, chopped
1 tsp salt
grated rind of 1 lime
4 garlic cloves, chopped
3 shallots, chopped
2 kaffir lime leaves, mid-rib removed,
    shredded
1 tbsp oil to blend

1 To make the curry paste, grind all the ingredients together in a large pestle and mortar, food processor or spice grinder. The paste will keep for up to 3 weeks in a sealed jar in the refrigerator.

2 Put a wok or large, heavy frying pan (skillet) over a high heat. Add the red curry paste and stir until fragrant. Reduce the heat.

3 Add the coconut milk, lime leaf, light soy sauce, baby corn, broccoli, beans and cashew nuts. Bring to the boil and simmer for about 10 minutes until the vegetables are cooked, but still firm.

4 Remove the lime leaf and stir in the basil leaves and coriander (cilantro). Serve over rice, garnished with peanuts.

VARIATION

Thai shops often have small, green, pea aubergines (eggplants) which have a very peppery taste, and are excellent when cooked in this dish. They can be quite firm and should be blanched before adding to the curry with the other vegetables.

GREEN CURRY WITH TEMPEH

There are three basic curries in Thai cuisine, of which the green curry is the hottest, red curry is medium and Massaman curry is the mildest. The green curry paste will keep for up to 3 weeks in the refrigerator. Serve over rice or noodles.

STEP 1

STEP 3

STEP 4

STEP 5

SERVES 4

1 tbsp sunflower oil
175 g/6 oz marinated or plain tempeh, cut into diamonds
6 spring onions (scallions), cut into 2.5 cm/1 inch pieces
150 ml/¹/₄ pint/²/₃ cup coconut milk
6 tbsp Green Curry Paste (see below)
grated rind of 1 lime
15 g/¹/₂ oz/¹/₄ cup fresh basil leaves
¹/₄ tsp liquid seasoning, such as Maggi

GREEN CURRY PASTE:
2 tsp coriander seeds
1 tsp cumin seeds
1 tsp black peppercorns
4 large green chillies, deseeded
2 shallots, quartered
2 garlic cloves, peeled
2 tbsp chopped fresh coriander (cilantro), including root and stalk
grated rind of 1 lime
1 tbsp roughly chopped galangal
1 tsp ground turmeric
salt
2 tbsp oil

TO GARNISH:
fresh coriander (cilantro) leaves
2 green chillies, sliced thinly

1 To make the green curry paste, grind together the coriander and cumin seeds and the peppercorns in a food processor or pestle and mortar.

2 Blend the remaining ingredients together and add the ground spice mixture. Store in a clean, dry jar for up to 3 weeks in the refrigerator, or freeze in a suitable container. Makes 6 tablespoons.

3 Heat the oil in a wok or large, heavy frying pan (skillet). Add the tempeh and stir over a high heat for about 2 minutes until sealed on all sides. Add the spring onions (scallions) and stir-fry for 1 minute. Remove the tempeh and spring onions (scallions) and reserve.

4 Put half the coconut milk into the wok or pan (skillet) and bring to the boil. Add the curry paste and lime rind, and cook until fragrant, about 1 minute. Add the reserved tempeh and spring onions (scallions).

5 Add the remaining coconut milk and simmer for 7–8 minutes. Stir in the basil leaves and liquid seasoning. Simmer for one more minute before serving, garnished with coriander (cilantro) and chillies.

MASSAMAN CURRIED RICE

Massaman paste is the mildest of Thai curry pastes, and owes its strong aroma to its Muslim origins. This is a deliciously rich curry.

STEP 1

SERVES 4

PASTE:
1 tsp coriander seeds
1 tsp cumin seeds
1 tsp ground cinnamon
1 tsp cloves
1 whole star anise
1 tsp cardamom pods
1 tsp white peppercorns
1 tbsp oil
6 shallots, chopped very roughly
6 garlic cloves, chopped very roughly
5 cm/2 inch piece lemon grass, sliced
4 fresh red chillies, deseeded and chopped
grated rind of 1 lime
1 tsp salt
1 tbsp chopped roast peanuts, to garnish

CURRY:
3 tbsp sunflower oil
250 g/8 oz/1 cup marinated tofu (bean
    curd), cut into 2.5 cm/1 inch cubes
125 g/4 oz green beans, cut into 2.5cm/
    1 inch lengths
1 kg/2 lb/6 cups cooked rice (300 g/
    10 oz/1¹/₂ cups raw weight)
3 shallots, diced finely and deep-fried
1 spring onion (scallion),chopped finely
2 tbsp chopped roast peanuts
1 tbsp lime juice

1 First, make the paste. Grind together the seeds and spices in a pestle and mortar or spice grinder.

2 Heat the oil in a wok or saucepan. Add the shallots, garlic and lemon grass. Cook over a low heat until soft, about 5 minutes, and then add the chilli and grind together with the dry spices. Stir in the lime rind and salt.

3 To make the curry, heat the oil in a wok or large, heavy frying pan (skillet). Cook the tofu (bean curd) over a high heat for 2 minutes to seal. Add the curry paste and beans, and stir. Add the rice and, using 2 spoons, lift and stir over a high heat for about 3 minutes.

4 Transfer to a warmed serving dish. Sprinkle with the deep-fried shallots, spring onion (scallion) and peanuts. Squeeze over the lime juice.

STEP 2

STEP 3

VARIATION

A variety of crunchy vegetables can be used in this dish. Celery, red (bell) peppers, broccoli, mangetout (snow peas) or shredded white cabbage can all be used very successfully.

STEP 3

STEP 1

STEP 2

STEP 3

STEP 5

AUBERGINE (EGGPLANT) & MUSHROOM SATAY WITH PEANUT SAUCE

Grilled, skewered vegetables are served with a satay sauce.

SERVES 4

8 wooden or metal skewers.
2 aubergines (eggplants), cut into 2.5 cm/
    1 inch pieces
175 g/6 oz chestnut (crimini) mushrooms

MARINADE:
1 tsp cumin seed
1 tsp coriander seed
2.5 cm/1 inch piece ginger root, grated
2 garlic cloves, crushed lightly
½ stalk lemon grass, chopped roughly
4 tbsp light soy sauce
8 tbsp sunflower oil
2 tbsp lemon juice

PEANUT SAUCE:
½ tsp cumin seed
½ tsp coriander seed
3 garlic cloves
1 small onion, quartered
1 tbsp lemon juice
1 tsp salt
½ red chilli, deseeded and sliced
120 ml/4 fl oz/½ cup coconut milk
250 g/8 oz/1 cup crunchy peanut butter
250 ml/8 fl oz/1 cup water

1 If using wooden skewers, soak in hand-hot water for 5 minutes. Thread the aubergine (eggplant) and mushroom on to the skewers.

2 To make the marinade, grind the cumin and coriander seeds, ginger, garlic and lemon grass. Put in a wok or a large frying pan (skillet). Stir over a high heat until fragrant. Remove from the heat and add the remaining marinade ingredients.

3 Place the skewers in a non-porous dish and spoon the marinade over the skewers. Leave to marinate for a minimum of 2 hours and up to 8 hours.

4 To make the peanut sauce, grind together the cumin and coriander seeds and the garlic. Switch on your food processor or blender and feed in the onion, or chop it finely by hand, then add to the cumin seed mixture. Add the rest of the ingredients, except the water.

5 Transfer to a saucepan and blend in the water. Bring to the boil and simmer until the required thickness is reached. Transfer to a serving bowl.

6 Place the skewers on a baking sheet (cookie sheet) and cook under a preheated very hot grill (broiler) for 15–20 minutes. Brush with the marinade frequently and turn once. Serve with the peanut sauce.

STEP 1

STEP 2

STEP 2

STEP 3

THREE MUSHROOMS IN COCONUT MILK

A filling and tasty main course dish served over rice or noodles.

SERVES 4

2 lemon grass stalks, sliced thinly
2 green chillies, deseeded and chopped finely
1 tbsp light soy sauce
2 garlic cloves, crushed
2 tbsp chopped fresh coriander (cilantro)
2 tbsp chopped fresh parsley
6 slices galangal, peeled
3 tbsp sunflower oil
1 aubergine (eggplant), cubed
60 g/2 oz/²/₃ cup oyster mushrooms
60 g/2 oz/²/₃ cup chestnut (crimini) mushrooms
60 g/2 oz/²/₃ cup field mushrooms, quartered if large
125 g/4 oz green beans, cut into 5 cm/ 2 inch lengths, blanched
300 ml/¹/₂ pint/ 1¹/₄ cups coconut milk
1 tbsp lemon juice
2 tbsp chopped roasted peanuts, to garnish

1 Grind together the lemon grass, chillies, soy sauce, garlic, coriander (cilantro), parsley and galangal in a large pestle and mortar or a food processor. Set aside.

2 Heat the sunflower oil in a wok or large, heavy frying pan (skillet). Add the aubergine (eggplant) and stir over a high heat for 3 minutes; then add the mushrooms, stir and add the beans. Cook for 3 minutes, stirring constantly. Add the ground spice paste.

3 Add the coconut milk and lemon juice to the pan, bring to the boil and simmer for 2 minutes.

4 Serve immediately over rice, and garnish with the roasted peanuts.

VARIATION

Any mixture of tasty mushrooms can be used in this recipe. If using dried mushrooms, use 15 g/¹/₂ oz/1 tbsp for every 60 g/2 oz/²/₃ cup fresh.

CHAPTER EIGHT

Vegetables

The recipes in this chapter are intended either as accompaniments for the main course dishes, or they can be served as versatile starters, buffet dishes and light snacks. The dishes are light and delicate as a complement to the richer textures and more complex flavours of the main course dishes.

An astonishing variety of vegetables are found in the markets of Thailand. Many of these vegetables can now be found in your local supermarket, speciality food stores or oriental supermarkets. Some things, sadly, you may not find, such as the many varieties of aubergine (eggplant) found in Thailand in every size, shape and colour – they have the appearance of peas, the colour of jewels and the shape of cucumbers. Walking around a Thai market is a revelation to every foreign visitor; the infinite variety of fresh raw produce looks spectacular piled high. But there are many delicious and authentic Thai dishes that can be made with imported goods, or with your own local produce.

Opposite: *A floating market at Damnoen Saduak, southwest of Bangkok.*

STEP 3

STEP 3

STEP 4

STEP 5

STIR-FRIED GREENS

This is an easy recipe to make as a quick accompaniment to a main course. The water chestnuts give a delicious crunch to the greens.

SERVES 4

1 tbsp sunflower oil
1 garlic clove, halved
2 spring onions (scallions), sliced finely
227 g/7½ oz can water chestnuts, drained
   and sliced finely (optional)
500 g/1 lb spinach, any tough stalks
   removed
1 tsp sherry vinegar
1 tsp light soy sauce
pepper

1 Heat the oil in a wok or large, heavy frying pan (skillet) over a high heat.

2 Add the garlic and cook, stirring, for 1 minute. If the garlic should brown, remove it immediately.

3 Add the spring onions (scallions) and water chestnuts, if using, and stir for 2–3 minutes. Add the spinach and stir.

4 Add the sherry vinegar, soy sauce and a sprinkling of pepper. Cook, stirring, until the spinach is tender. Remove the garlic.

5 Use a slotted spoon in order to drain off the excess liquid and serve immediately.

TIPS

These stir-fried greens are delicious served as an accompaniment to the Red Curry with Cashews (see page 102).
   Several types of oriental greens (for example, choi sam and pak choi) are widely available and any of these can be successfully substituted for the spinach.

STEP 1

STEP 2

STEP 3

STEP 4

CAULIFLOWER WITH THAI SPINACH

This is a delicious way to cook cauliflower – even without the spinach!

SERVES 4

175 g/6 oz cauliflower, cut into florets
1 garlic clove
$\frac{1}{2}$ tsp turmeric
1 tbsp coriander (cilantro) root or stem
1 tbsp sunflower oil
*2 spring onions (scallions), cut into
   2.5 cm/1 inch pieces*
*125 g/4 oz Thai spinach, tough stalks
   removed, or oriental greens*
1 tsp yellow mustard seeds

1 Blanch the cauliflower, rinse in cold running water and drain. Set aside.

2 Grind the garlic, turmeric and coriander (cilantro) root or stem together in a pestle and mortar or spice grinder.

3 Heat the oil in a wok or large, heavy frying pan (skillet). Add the spring onions (scallions) and stir over a high heat for 2 minutes. Add the Thai spinach, or greens, and stir for 1 minute. Set aside.

4 Return the wok or frying pan (skillet) to the heat and add the mustard seeds. Stir until they start to

pop, then add the turmeric mixture and the cauliflower, and stir until all the cauliflower is coated.

5 Serve with the spinach or greens on a warmed serving plate.

SUBSTITUTES

Oriental greens are now available in many of the larger supermarkets; however, spinach or chard is equally good with the cauliflower.

MIXED VEGETABLES IN COCONUT MILK

This is a deliciously crunchy way to prepare a mixture of vegetables.

STEP 1

SERVES 4–6

1 red chilli, deseeded and chopped
1 tsp coriander seeds
1 tsp cumin seeds
2 garlic cloves, crushed
juice of 1 lime
250 ml/8 fl oz/1 cup coconut milk
125 g/4 oz/2 cups bean-sprouts
125 g/4 oz/2 cups white cabbage,
  shredded
125 g/4 oz mangetout (snow peas),
  trimmed
125 g/4 oz/1¼ cups carrots, sliced
  thinly
125 g/4 oz/1¼ cups cauliflower florets
3 tbsp peanut butter
grated or shaved coconut, to garnish

1 Grind together the chilli, coriander and cumin seeds, garlic and lime juice in a pestle and mortar or food processor.

2 Put into a medium saucepan and heat gently until fragrant, about 1 minute. Add the coconut milk and stir until just about to boil.

3 Meanwhile, mix all the vegetables together in a large bowl.

4 Stir the peanut butter into the coconut mixture and combine with the vegetables. Sprinkle over slivers of grated or shaved coconut. Serve immediately.

STEP 2

STEP 3

TIPS

If you prefer, the cauliflower, carrots and mangetout (snow peas) can be blanched before being mixed with the dressing, to give them less bite.

This dish is ideal as a buffet dish as the quantity of dressing is quite sparse, and is only intended to coat, so you don't need too much of it to cover a large bowlful of vegetables.

STEP 4

STEP 2

STEP 3

STEP 3

STEP 4

CARROT & CORIANDER (CILANTRO) SALAD

This is a tangy, crunchy salad, which is popular with everyone. It makes an ideal accompaniment to Aubergine (Eggplant) & Mushroom Satay with Peanut Sauce (see page 108).

SERVES 4

4 large carrots
2 celery sticks, cut into matchsticks
2 tbsp roughly chopped fresh coriander
   (cilantro)

DRESSING:
1 tbsp sesame oil
1$\frac{1}{2}$ tbsp rice vinegar
$\frac{1}{2}$ tsp sugar
$\frac{1}{2}$ tsp salt

1 To create flower-shaped carrot slices, as shown, cut several grooves lengthways along each carrot before slicing it.

2 Slice each carrot into very thin slices, using the slicing cutter of a grater.

3 Combine the carrot, celery and coriander (cilantro) in a bowl. Combine the dressing ingredients thoroughly.

4 Just before serving, toss the carrot, celery and coriander mixture in the dressing and transfer to a serving dish.

GARNISHES

You can make this attractive salad look even more appealing with the addition of a simple garnish. Cut very fine strips of carrot with a vegetable peeler and curl into a spiral, or drop in iced water for a few minutes to make them curl up. Alternatively you could make very thin cuts through a chunk of celery from the top almost to the bottom, and leave in iced water until the fronds curl up.

SESAME OIL

Sesame oil is a very aromatic oil used in small quantities in a lot of oriental cooking, to impart a special flavour to salad dressings and sauces. If it is not available, you can substitute any high quality oil, though the dressing will not have the distinctive Thai flavour.

STEP 1

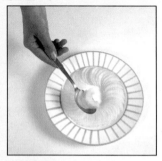

STEP 2

STEP 3

STEP 5

CUCUMBER SALAD

*This is a very refreshing accompaniment to any main dish and is an
excellent 'cooler' for curries. Alternatively, it can be served simply as a
salad on a buffet.*

SERVES 4

$^1\!/_2$ cucumber
1 tbsp rice vinegar
2 tbsp sugar
2 tbsp hot water
$^1\!/_2$ tsp salt
1 small shallot, sliced thinly

1 Peel the cucumber, halve it
lengthways, and deseed it, using a
teaspoon or a melon baller.

2 Slice the cucumber thinly, and
arrange the cucumber slices on a
serving plate.

3 To make the dressing, combine the
vinegar, sugar and salt in a bowl.
Pour on the hot water and stir until the
sugar has dissolved.

4 Pour the dressing evenly over the
cucumber slices.

5 Sprinkle the shallot slices over the
cucumber. Chill the salad before
serving.

RICE VINEGAR

There are two kinds of rice vinegar, each
of which is less acidic than Western
vinegars. Red vinegar is made from
fermented rice, and has a dark colour and
depth of flavour. White rice vinegar is
distilled from rice wine and has a stronger
flavour than red vinegar. Because of this
distinctive but subtle flavour, white rice
vinegar is preferred by many Western
cooks. If it is unavailable, you can use
white wine vinegar or cider vinegar.

CUCUMBERS

Some people dislike the bitter taste that
cucumbers can have – peeling off the skin
and deseeding the cucumber often
eliminates this problem.
    Using a melon baller is the neatest
method of deseeding a cucumber,
although a rounded teaspoon will do
instead.

STEP 1

STEP 2

STEP 3

STEP 4

GRAPEFRUIT & COCONUT SALAD

This salad is deceptive – it is in fact quite filling, even though it looks very light.

SERVES 4

125 g/4 oz/1 cup grated coconut
2 tsp light soy sauce
2 tbsp lime juice
2 tbsp water
2 tsp sunflower oil
1 garlic clove, halved
1 onion, chopped finely
2 large ruby grapefruits, peeled and
  segmented
90 g/ 3 oz/ 1½ cups alfalfa sprouts

1 Toast the coconut in a dry frying pan (skillet), stirring constantly, until golden brown, about 3 minutes. Transfer to a bowl.

2 Add the light soy sauce, lime juice and water.

3 Heat the oil in a saucepan and fry the garlic and onion until soft. Stir the onion into the coconut mixture. Remove the garlic.

4 Divide the grapefruit segments between 4 plates. Sprinkle each with a quarter of the alfalfa sprouts and spoon over a quarter of the coconut mixture.

ALFALFA SPROUTS

Alfalfa sprouts can be bought in trays or packets from most supermarkets, but you can easily grow your own, if you like to have a constant and cheap supply.

Soak a couple of tablespoons of alfalfa seeds overnight in warm water. Drain the seeds and place them in a jam jar, or a sprouting tray if you have one. Cover the neck of the jar with a piece of muslin (cheesecloth) or fine netting. Leave in a dark, warm place. Once a day, fill the jar with warm water, then turn it upside down and allow the water to drain out through the muslin. After 3 or 4 days, the seeds will be ready to eat.

You can sprout almost any seeds and beans in this way, including mung beans, which turn into bean-sprouts, and are usually much crunchier than the shop-bought variety.

CELERY & GREEN (BELL) PEPPER WITH SESAME DRESSING

A very elegant and light salad which will complement rice and noodle dishes beautifully.

STEP 1

STEP 2

STEP 3

STEP 5

SERVES 4

125 g/4 oz/2 cups bean-sprouts
1½ tbsp chopped coriander (cilantro)
3 tbsp fresh lime juice
½ tsp mild chilli powder
1 tsp sugar
½ tsp salt
3 celery sticks, cut into 2.5 cm/1 inch pieces
1 large green (bell) pepper, cored, deseeded and chopped
1 large tart dessert apple
2 tbsp sesame seeds, to garnish

1 Rinse and drain the bean-sprouts. Pick them over and remove any that seem a little brown or limp – it is essential that they are fresh and crunchy for this recipe.

2 To make the dressing, combine the coriander (cilantro), lime juice, chilli powder, sugar and salt in a small bowl and mix thoroughly.

3 In a larger bowl, combine the celery, (bell) pepper, bean-sprouts and apple.

4 To prepare the garnish, toast the sesame seeds in a dry frying pan (skillet) until they just start to colour.

5 Stir the dressing into the mixed vegetables just before serving. Garnish with the toasted sesame seeds.

FRESH INGREDIENTS

Keeping each ingredient as fresh and crunchy as possible will make all the difference to the appearance and taste of this elegant salad. Choose the freshest, whitest bean-sprouts, and discard any coriander (cilantro) leaves that are limp or yellowed.

APPLES

To prevent the apple slices from going brown, place them in a little lemon juice and water as soon as you have cut them, and turn them in the juice to ensure they are covered.

CHAPTER NINE

Buffet Dishes

Thai cuisine lends itself brilliantly to party food – it is always colourful, exquisitely presented and made for sharing.

Any Thai meal eaten in an ordinary Thai home will be presented as three or four dishes or more, arranged around a central steaming hot bowl of fragrant rice. Each diner takes some rice and some of each dish in turn, all meant to be savoured with the rice. However, a Thai meal eaten in a rather grander home or palace will be in the same format, but the dishes will be chosen from the slightly more elaborate 'Royal Cuisine' which is the origin of the Little Golden Parcels and the Fried Rice in Pineapple.

It is in a 'Royal' meal that one will see the most elaborate garnishes. With the aid of a very small, very sharp knife, and several years' experience, the royal vegetable carver will transform carrots, onions, apples and chilli into beautiful blossoms, birds, lilies and fishes. You can emulate this with a simple spring onion (scallion) tassel or chilli flowers to garnish a party buffet, and, with practice, carrot flowers or potato birds.

Opposite: *A banana seller in Chiang Mai.*

STEP 1

STEP 2

STEP 3

STEP 3

LITTLE GOLDEN PARCELS

These little parcels will draw admiring gasps from your guests, but they are fairly simple to prepare.

MAKES 30

1 garlic clove, crushed
1 tsp chopped coriander (cilantro) root
1 tsp pepper
250 g/8 oz/1 cup boiled mashed potato
175 g/6 oz/1 cup water chestnuts, chopped
    finely
1 tsp grated ginger root
2 tbsp ground roast peanuts
2 tsp light soy sauce
$^{1}/_{2}$ tsp salt
$^{1}/_{2}$ tsp sugar
30 wonton sheets, defrosted
1 tsp cornflour (cornstarch), made into a
    paste with a little water
vegetable oil for deep-frying
fresh chives, to garnish
sweet chilli sauce, to serve

1 Combine all the ingredients thoroughly, except the wonton sheets, cornflour (cornstarch) and oil.

2 Keeping the remainder of the wonton sheets covered with a damp cloth, lay 4 sheets out on a work surface (counter). Put a teaspoonful of the mixture on each.

3 Drizzle a line of the cornflour (cornstarch) paste around each

sheet, about 1 cm/$^{1}/_{2}$ inch from the edge. Bring all 4 corners to the centre and press together to form little bags. Continue the process until all the wonton sheets are used.

4 Meanwhile, heat 5 cm/2 inches of the oil in a deep saucepan until a light haze appears on top and lower the parcels in, in batches of 3. Fry until golden brown, and remove with a slotted spoon, to drain on paper towels.

5 Tie a chive around the neck of each bag to garnish, and serve with a sweet chilli sauce for dipping.

WONTON SHEETS

If wonton sheets are not available, use spring roll sheets or filo pastry, and cut the large squares down to about 10 cm/ 4 inches square.

SON-IN-LAW EGGS

This recipe is supposedly so called because it is an easy dish for a son-in-law to cook to impress his new mother-in-law!

STEP 1

STEP 2

STEP 3

STEP 4

SERVES 4

6 eggs, hard-boiled (hard-cooked) and
    shelled
4 tbsp sunflower oil
1 onion, sliced thinly
2 fresh red chillies, sliced
2 tbsp sugar
1 tbsp water
2 tsp tamarind pulp
1 tbsp liquid seasoning, such as Maggi

1 Prick the hard-boiled (hard-cooked) eggs 2 or 3 times with a cocktail stick (toothpick).

2 Heat the oil in a wok or large, heavy frying pan (skillet) and fry the eggs until crispy and golden. Drain on paper towels.

3 Halve the eggs lengthways and put on a serving dish.

4 Reserve 1 tablespoon of the oil, pour off the rest, then heat the tablespoonful in the wok or pan (skillet). Cook the onion and chillies over a high heat until golden and slightly crisp. Drain on paper towels.

5 Combine the sugar, water, tamarind pulp and liquid seasoning. Simmer for 5 minutes until thickened.

6 Pour the sauce over the eggs and spoon over the onion and chillies. Serve immediately with rice.

TAMARIND PULP

Tamarind pulp is sold in oriental stores, and is quite sour. If it is not available, use twice the amount of lemon juice in its place.

PERFECT EGGS

When hard-boiling (hard-cooking) eggs, stir the water gently one way, then the other, and you will have beautifully centred yolks.

STEP 2

STEP 2

STEP 3

STEP 4

FRIED RICE IN PINEAPPLE BOATS

This looks very impressive on a party buffet, and has a mild, pleasant flavour, so everyone can sample it. However, if you simply want to serve it as a main course, quarter the pineapple and carry on with the recipe.

SERVES 4–6

1 large pineapple
1 tbsp sunflower oil
1 garlic clove, crushed
1 small onion, diced
$\frac{1}{2}$ celery stick, sliced
1 tsp coriander seeds, ground
1 tsp cumin seeds, ground
150 g/ 5 oz/ 1$\frac{1}{2}$ cups button mushrooms, sliced
250 g/ 8 oz/ 1$\frac{1}{3}$ cups cooked rice
2 tbsp light soy sauce
$\frac{1}{2}$ tsp sugar
$\frac{1}{2}$ tsp salt
30 g/ 1 oz/ $\frac{1}{4}$ cup cashew nuts

TO GARNISH:
1 spring onion (scallion), sliced finely
fresh coriander (cilantro) leaves
mint sprig

1 Halve the pineapple lengthways and cut out the flesh to make 2 boat-shaped shells. Cut the flesh into cubes and reserve 125 g/4 oz/1 cup to use in this recipe. (Any remaining pineapple cubes can be served separately.)

2 Heat the oil in a wok or large, heavy frying pan (skillet). Cook the garlic, onion and celery over a high heat, stirring constantly, for 2 minutes. Stir in the coriander and cumin seeds, and the mushrooms.

3 Add the pineapple cubes and cooked rice to the pan and stir well. Stir in the soy sauce, sugar, salt and cashew nuts.

4 Using 2 spoons, lift and stir the rice for about 4 minutes until it is thoroughly heated.

5 Spoon the rice mixture into the pineapple boats. Garnish with spring onion (scallion), coriander (cilantro) leaves and chopped mint.

PINEAPPLE

The remaining pineapple flesh can be combined with paw-paw (papaya) and mango for an exotic fruit salad, which is delicious served in pineapple boats or a watermelon basket. For instructions on how to make a watermelon basket, see page 138.

SPRING ROLLS

The Thai spring rolls are not as heavy as the Chinese version and are ideal as canapés with drinks or as part of a finger buffet. The easiest way to break the rice vermicelli is to crush it in the packet before opening it to weigh it.

STEP 1

SERVES 6

2 tbsp plain (all-purpose) flour
150 ml/¼ pint/⅔ cup water
60 g/2 oz/½ cup dried rice vermicelli, broken into small pieces
1 garlic clove, crushed
1 green (bell) pepper, chopped finely
1 celery stick, chopped finely
2 spring onions (scallions), chopped finely
125 g/4 oz/1⅓ cups button mushrooms, sliced finely
2 tsp liquid seasoning, such as Maggi
½ tsp sugar
8 frozen spring roll sheets, 25 cm/10 inches square, defrosted
oil for frying

SAUCE:
4 tbsp rice vinegar
4 tbsp sugar
½ tsp salt
1 small red chilli, chopped finely

1 Mix the flour and water together over a low heat, stirring constantly until thick and translucent. Pour into a saucer and set aside.

2 Blanch the rice vermicelli in boiling water for 30 seconds. Stir and drain. Set aside.

3 Heat 1 tablespoon of the oil in a wok or large, heavy frying pan (skillet) over a high heat. Add the garlic, green (bell) pepper, celery, spring onion (scallion) and button mushrooms. Stir until the vegetables are softened. Add the liquid seasoning and sugar. Remove from the heat and transfer to paper towels to drain briefly. Stir into the rice vermicelli.

4 Cut the first spring roll sheet into 4 squares. Place about 2 teaspoons of the vermicelli mixture in the centre of each square. Fold 3 corners inwards like an envelope, and roll up to the fourth corner. Dab a little of the flour and water paste on this corner to seal. At this stage the spring rolls can be chilled or frozen for later use.

5 Heat the oil in a wok or deep-fat fryer until a light haze appears on top. Have ready a plate lined with paper towels. Deep-fry the spring rolls in batches until golden brown. Drain well on the paper towels.

6 To make the sauce, boil all the ingredients together, stirring frequently until the sauce thickens, about 5 minutes. Pour into a small bowl or saucer. Serve with the spring rolls.

STEP 3

STEP 4

STEP 6

137

STEP 1

STEP 3

STEP 3

STEP 4

MANGO SALAD

A version of this popular salad is sold all over Thailand. It is an unusual combination but works well as long as the mango is very unripe. Paw-paw can be used instead, if you prefer. The components of the salad can be prepared ahead, but should not be assembled until just before serving, so that the flavours remain distinct.

SERVES 4

1 lollo biondo lettuce, or any crunchy lettuce
15 g/$^1/_2$ oz coriander (cilantro) leaves
1 large unripe mango, peeled and cut into
   long thin shreds
1 small red chilli, deseeded and chopped
   finely
2 shallots, chopped finely
2 tbsp lemon juice
1 tbsp light soy sauce
6 roasted canned chestnuts, quartered

1 Line a serving plate with the lettuce and coriander (cilantro).

2 Soak the mango briefly in cold water, in order to remove any syrup, while you prepare the dressing.

3 Combine the chilli, shallots, lemon juice and soy sauce.

4 Drain the mango, combine with the chestnuts and spoon on to the serving plate.

5 Pour over the dressing and serve immediately.

WATERMELON BASKET

This would look wonderful if served in a watermelon basket. To make a watermelon basket, stand a watermelon on one end on a level surface. Holding a knife level and in one place, turn the watermelon on its axis so that the knife marks an even line all around the middle. Mark a 2.5 cm/1 inch wide handle across the top and through the centre stem, joining the middle line at either end. (If you prefer a zigzag finish, mark the shape to be cut at this point before any cuts are made, to ensure even zigzags.)

Take a sharp knife and, following the marks made for the handle, make the first vertical cut. Then cut down the other side of the handle. Now follow the middle line and make your straight or zigzag cut, taking care that the knife is always pointing towards the centre of the watermelon, and is level with the work surface (counter), as this ensures that when you reach the handle cuts, the cut-out piece of melon will pull away cleanly. Hollow out the flesh with a spoon, leaving a clean edge, and fill as required.

STEP 1

STEP 1

STEP 2

STEP 3

SWEETCORN PATTIES

These are a delicious addition to any party buffet, and very simple to prepare. Serve with a sweet chilli sauce.

MAKES 12

325 g/11 oz can sweetcorn, drained
1 onion, chopped finely
1 tsp curry powder
1 garlic clove, crushed
1 tsp ground coriander
2 spring onions (scallions), chopped
3 tbsp plain (all-purpose) flour
$^1\!/_2$ tsp baking powder
salt
1 large egg
4 tbsp sunflower oil

1 Mash the drained sweetcorn lightly in a medium-sized bowl. Add all the remaining ingredients, except for the oil, one at a time, stirring after each addition.

2 Heat the sunflower oil in a frying pan (skillet). Drop tablespoonfuls of the mixture carefully on to the hot oil, far enough apart for them not to run into each other as they cook.

3 Cook for 4–5 minutes, turning each patty once, until they are golden brown and firm. Take care not to turn them too soon, or they will break up in the pan.

4 Remove from the pan with a slice and drain on paper towels. Serve quickly while still warm.

PRESENTATION

To make this dish more attractive, you can serve the patties on large leaves, like those shown. Be sure to cut the spring onions (scallions) on the slant, as shown, for a more elegant appearance.

TIME SAVER

The mixture can be made in advance and will keep in the refrigerator for up to 2 days.

3

**THAI
SIDE DISHES**

CHAPTER TEN

Rice & Noodles

Rice and noodles form the backbone of Thai cookery and are usually the main component of the central dish, as well as appearing in side dishes and sometimes soups. Experiment with the recipes in this chapter to get a taste of the many ways in which rice and noodles feature in this imaginative and colourful cuisine.

Rice can make an appearance at the Thai table as a simple, plainly cooked side dish, or it can be a marvellous mixture of colours and flavours, full of surprises to the palate. Just try the recipe for Chilli Fried Rice to give a glorious example. 'Sticky' or glutinous rice is a mainstay in Thailand too, where it is used in desserts. One of the most popular snacks is Mangoes with Sticky Rice – served in banana leaves as a convenient and natural form of wrapping.

Noodles tend to be used in stir-fries in Thailand. In this chapter you will find two typical recipes for noodles, in which everything is quickly cooked in a wok or frying pan (skillet) to retain all the colour, flavour and goodness of the ingredients.

Look out for different varieties of rice and noodles in your supermarket – you'll be surprised at the range. And if you get the chance, visit a supplier of oriental foods to stock up your storecupboard with some of the more unusual types.

Opposite: *A small village in the hills of Thailand, not far from Chiang Mai.*

STEP 1

STEP 2

STEP 3

STEP 4

CRISPY NOODLES WITH CORIANDER (CILANTRO) & CUCUMBER

These crispy noodles will add a delicious crunch to your Thai meal.

SERVES 4

250 g/8 oz rice noodles
oil for deep-frying
2 garlic cloves, chopped finely
8 spring onions (scallions), trimmed and
    chopped finely
1 small red or green chilli, deseeded and
    chopped finely
2 tbsp fish sauce
2 tbsp light soy sauce
2 tbsp lime or lemon juice
2 tbsp molasses sugar

TO GARNISH:
spring onions (scallions), shredded
cucumber, sliced thinly
fresh chillies
fresh coriander (cilantro)

1 Break the noodles into smaller pieces with your hands.

2 Heat the oil for deep-frying in a wok or large frying pan (skillet). Add small batches of the noodles and fry them until pale golden brown and puffed up. Make sure that the oil is hot enough, or they will be tough. As each batch cooks, lift the noodles out with a perforated spoon on to paper towels.

3 When all the noodles are cooked, carefully pour off the oil into a separate container, then return 3 tablespoons of it to the wok or frying pan (skillet). Add the garlic, spring onions (scallions) and chilli and stir-fry for about 2 minutes.

4 Mix together the fish sauce, soy sauce, lime or lemon juice and sugar. Add to the wok or frying pan (skillet) and cook for about 2 minutes until the sugar has dissolved. Tip all the noodles back into the wok or frying pan (skillet) and toss lightly to coat with the sauce mixture. Avoid breaking them up too much.

5 Serve the noodles garnished with shredded spring onions (scallions), thinly sliced cucumber, chillies and fresh coriander (cilantro).

VARIATION

Stir-fry some uncooked peeled prawns (shrimp) or chopped raw chicken with the spring onions (scallions) and garlic in step 3. Cook for an extra 3–4 minutes to make sure they are thoroughly cooked.

STEP 1

STEP 2

STEP 3

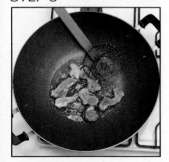

STEP 4

SPICY CHICKEN & NOODLE SALAD

Strips of lean chicken are coated in a delicious spicy mixture, then stir-fried with noodles and served on a bed of salad in this quick and easy recipe.

SERVES 4

1 tsp finely grated fresh ginger root
1/2 tsp Chinese five-spice powder
1 tbsp plain (all-purpose) flour
1/2 tsp chilli powder
350 g/12 oz boned chicken breast, skinned
    and sliced thinly
60 g/2 oz rice noodles
125 g/4 oz/1 1/2 cups Chinese leaves or hard
    white cabbage, shredded finely
7 cm/3 inch piece cucumber, sliced finely
1 large carrot, pared thinly
1 tbsp olive oil
2 tbsp lime or lemon juice
2 tbsp sesame oil
salt and pepper

TO GARNISH:
lemon or lime slices
fresh coriander (cilantro) leaves

1 Mix together the ginger, five-spice powder, flour and chilli powder in a shallow mixing bowl. Season with salt and pepper. Add the strips of chicken and roll in the mixture until well coated.

2 Put the noodles into a large bowl and cover with warm water. Leave them to soak for about 5 minutes, then drain them well.

3 Mix together the Chinese leaves or cabbage, cucumber and carrot and arrange them in a salad bowl. Whisk together the olive oil and lime or lemon juice, season with a little salt and pepper and use to dress the salad.

4 Heat the sesame oil in a wok or frying pan (skillet) and add the chicken. Stir-fry for 5–6 minutes until well browned and crispy on the outside. Remove from the wok or frying pan (skillet) with a perforated spoon and drain on paper towels.

5 Add the noodles to the wok or frying pan (skillet) and stir-fry for 3–4 minutes until heated through. Mix with the chicken and pile on top of the salad. Serve garnished with lime or lemon slices and coriander (cilantro) leaves.

TIPS

The easiest way to pare the carrot into fine strips is to use a potato peeler.
    A few peanuts or cashew nuts, quickly stir-fried in a little sesame oil, add extra crunch and flavour to this salad.

STEP 1

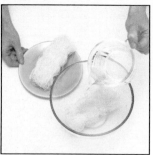

STEP 2

STEP 3

STEP 4

CELLOPHANE NOODLES WITH SHRIMPS & BEAN-SPROUTS

Cellophane or 'glass' noodles are made from mung beans. They are sold dried, so they need soaking before use.

SERVES 4

2 tbsp light soy sauce
1 tbsp lime or lemon juice
1 tbsp fish sauce
125 g/4 oz firm tofu (bean curd), cut into chunks
125 g/4 oz cellophane noodles
2 tbsp sesame oil
4 shallots, sliced finely
2 garlic cloves, crushed
1 small red chilli, deseeded and chopped finely
2 celery sticks, sliced finely
2 carrots, sliced finely
125 g/4 oz/²/₃ cup cooked, peeled shrimps (small shrimp)
60 g/2 oz/1 cup bean-sprouts

TO GARNISH:
carrot slices
celery leaves
fresh chillies

1 Mix together the soy sauce, lime or lemon juice and fish sauce in a shallow bowl. Add the tofu (bean curd) cubes and toss them in the mixture. Cover and set aside for 15 minutes.

2 Put the noodles into a large bowl and cover with warm water. Leave them to soak for about 5 minutes, and then drain them well.

3 Heat the sesame oil in a wok or large frying pan (skillet). Add the shallots, garlic and chilli and stir-fry for 1 minute. Add the celery and carrots, and stir-fry for a further 2–3 minutes.

4 Tip the drained noodles into the wok or frying pan (skillet) and cook, stirring, for 2 minutes, then add the shrimps, bean-sprouts and tofu (bean curd) with the soy sauce mixture. Cook over a medium-high heat for 2–3 minutes until heated through.

5 Transfer to a serving dish and garnish with carrot slices, celery leaves and chillies.

SHRIMPS

For speed and convenience, use canned shrimps, but make sure that you drain them well first.

CHILLI FRIED RICE

Not so much a side dish as a meal in itself, this delicious fried rice can be served on its own or as an accompaniment to many Thai dishes.

STEP 1

SERVES 4

250 g/8 oz/generous 1 cup long-grain rice
4 tbsp vegetable oil
2 garlic cloves, chopped finely
1 small red chilli, deseeded and chopped
   finely
8 spring onions (scallions), trimmed and
   sliced finely
1 tbsp Red Curry Paste (see page 102),or
   2 tsp chilli sauce
1 red (bell) pepper, cored, deseeded and
   chopped
90 g/3 oz/³/₄ cup dwarf green beans,
   chopped
250 g/8 oz/1¹/₂ cups cooked peeled prawns
   (shrimp) or chopped cooked chicken
2 tbsp fish sauce

TO GARNISH:
cucumber slices
shredded spring onion (scallion)

1 Cook the rice in plenty of boiling, lightly salted water for about 12 minutes until tender. Drain, rinse with cold water and drain thoroughly.

2 Heat the vegetable oil in a wok or large frying pan (skillet) and add the garlic. Fry gently for 2 minutes until golden. Add the chilli and spring onions

STEP 2

(scallions) and cook, stirring, for 3–4 minutes.

3 Add the Thai curry paste or chilli sauce to the wok or frying pan (skillet) and fry for 1 minute, then add the red (bell) pepper and green beans. Stir-fry briskly for 2 minutes.

4 Tip the cooked rice into the wok or frying pan (skillet) and add the prawns (shrimp) or chicken. Stir-fry over a medium-high heat for 4–5 minutes until the rice is hot.

5 Serve garnished with cucumber slices and shredded spring onion (scallion).

STEP 3

RICE

Cook the rice the day before if you can remember – it will give an even better result. Alternatively, use rice left over from another dish to make this recipe.

   Remember to cool any leftover rice quickly, then cover and refrigerate – it looks very innocent, but can be a cause of food poisoning if left out for any length of time in a warm environment.

STEP 4

STEP 2

STEP 3

STEP 4

STEP 5

STIR-FRIED NOODLES WITH THAI HOT SAUCE

This dish, like many Thai recipes, is very quick and simple to make. All the ingredients are cooked together in a wok, so there's very little washing-up to do!

SERVES 4

125 g/4 oz rice noodles
2 tbsp sesame oil
1 large garlic clove, crushed
125 g/4 oz pork fillet (tenderloin), sliced
  into strips
125 g/4 oz /²/₃ cup large prawns (shrimp),
  peeled and deveined
15 g/¹/₂ oz/ 1 tbsp dried shrimp (optional)
60 g/2 oz /¹/₂ cup white radish (mooli),
  grated
2 tbsp fish sauce
2 tbsp dark muscovado sugar
2 tbsp lime or lemon juice
60 g/2 oz/ 1 cup bean-sprouts
30 g/ 1 oz/¹/₄ cup peanuts, chopped
3–4 tbsp Thai hot sauce, to serve

TO GARNISH:
2 shallots, sliced
fresh coriander (cilantro) leaves

1 Put the noodles into a large bowl and cover them with just-boiled water. Leave to soak for 15 minutes.

2 Heat the oil in a wok or large frying pan (skillet) and add the garlic, stir-frying for 2 minutes until golden brown. Add the strips of pork and stir-fry for a further 4–5 minutes.

3 Add the prawns (shrimp), dried shrimp (if using) and white radish (mooli) to the wok or frying pan (skillet) and stir-fry briskly for 2 minutes.

4 Stir in the fish sauce, sugar and lime or lemon juice.

5 Drain the noodles well and stir into the wok or frying pan (skillet) with the bean-sprouts and peanuts. Cook for 2–3 minutes, then serve.

6 Drizzle the Thai hot sauce over the noodles and garnish with the sliced shallot and coriander (cilantro) leaves.

VARIATIONS

If you have a good local supplier of oriental foods, buy some pickled white radish and use it instead of fresh. About 2 tablespoons will be enough.

Vary this recipe to suit your taste – the only rule is that there are no rules! Chicken makes a good alternative to pork, and if you love hot food, add 1–2 chopped fresh chillies. Chilli sauce can be used in place of the Thai hot sauce.

STEP 1

STEP 2

STEP 3

STEP 4

MANGOES WITH STICKY RICE

This traditional South-East Asian dessert has to be included in this book, as every Thai cook knows how to make it, and it will round off any Thai meal perfectly.

SERVES 4

125 g/4 oz/generous ½ cup glutinous (sticky) rice
250 ml/8 fl oz/1 cup coconut milk
60 g/2 oz /⅓ cup light muscovado sugar
½ tsp salt
1 tsp sesame seeds, toasted
4 ripe mangoes, peeled, halved, stoned (pitted) and sliced

1 Put the rice into a colander and rinse well with plenty of cold water until the water runs clear. Transfer the rice to a large bowl, cover with cold water and leave to soak overnight, or for at least 12 hours. Drain well.

2 Line a bamboo basket or steamer with muslin (cheesecloth) or finely woven cotton cloth. Add the rice and steam over a pan of gently simmering water for about 40 minutes until the rice is tender. Remove from the heat and transfer the rice to a bowl.

3 Reserve 4 tablespoons of the coconut milk and put the remainder into a small saucepan with the sugar and salt. Heat and simmer gently for about 8 minutes until reduced by about one third.

4 Pour the coconut milk mixture over the rice, fluffing up the rice so that the mixture is absorbed. Set aside for 10–15 minutes.

5 Pack the rice into individual moulds and then invert them on to serving plates. Pour a little reserved coconut milk over each mound and sprinkle with the sesame seeds. Arrange the sliced mango on the plates and serve, decorated with pieces of mango cut into shapes with tiny cutters.

STICKY RICE

Glutinous or sticky rice is available from stockists of Thai ingredients, although you can try making this recipe with short-grain pudding rice instead.

COCONUT MILK

Canned coconut milk is widely available from supermarkets, or you can buy packets of coconut cream, which can be mixed with milk or water to make coconut milk. Dried coconut milk, which can be reconstituted with water, is also available.

CHAPTER ELEVEN

Fish & Seafood

Thousands of miles of coastline surround Thailand, and the country has many inland rivers and waterways, so it comes as no surprise to know that fish and seafood are extremely popular in Thai cookery. Being so cheap and plentiful, they are the main source of protein in the Thai diet. There is an amazing variety of fish and seafood constantly available, and no shortage of wonderful ways in which to cook it.

This chapter offers a tiny handful of recipes that use fish and seafood in side dishes – a taster of some of the best ways to sample some of Thailand's favourite food. Try, for example, the tasty Crab-meat Cakes, the King Prawns (Jumbo Shrimp) in Red Curry Sauce, or the Kaffir Lime Mussels with Lemon Grass.

When choosing fresh fish and seafood, always make sure that you buy from a reputable supermarket or fishmonger. Ask for advice when making your choice – if the fishmonger knows his or her business well, he or she will be able to help you. And don't forget to ask for help in preparing the catch. An expert fishmonger will deal with a pound or two of fresh squid far quicker than you can!

Opposite: *Thai fishermen sell their wares straight from the boat at a floating market in Saduak.*

STEP 1

STEP 2

STEP 3

STEP 5

PRAWNS (SHRIMP) WITH HOT & SWEET DIPPING SAUCE

Uncooked or 'green' prawns (shrimp) are speared on wooden skewers, brushed with a sesame oil, lime juice and fresh coriander (cilantro) baste, then grilled (broiled) until cooked. Enjoy their succulent flavour!

SERVES 4

wooden skewers soaked in warm water for 20 minutes
500 g/1 lb/2½ cups uncooked prawns (shrimp)
3 tbsp sesame oil
2 tbsp lime juice
1 tbsp chopped fresh coriander (cilantro)
sprigs of fresh coriander (cilantro), to garnish

SAUCE:
4 tbsp light malt vinegar
2 tbsp Thai fish sauce or light soy sauce
2 tbsp water
2 tbsp light muscovado sugar
2 garlic cloves, crushed
2 tsp grated fresh ginger root
1 red chilli, deseeded and chopped finely
2 tbsp chopped fresh coriander (cilantro)
salt

1 Peel the prawns (shrimp), leaving the tails intact. Remove the black vein that runs along the back of each one, then skewer the prawns (shrimp) on to the wooden skewers.

2 Mix together the sesame oil, lime juice and chopped coriander (cilantro) in a shallow bowl. Lay the skewered prawns (shrimp) in this mixture. Cover and chill for 30 minutes, turning once, so that the prawns (shrimp) absorb the marinade.

3 Meanwhile, make the sauce. Heat the vinegar, fish sauce or soy sauce, water, sugar and salt until boiling. Remove from the heat and leave to cool.

4 Mix together the garlic, ginger, chilli and coriander (cilantro) in a small serving bowl. Add the cooled vinegar mixture and stir together.

5 Place the prawns (shrimp) on a foil-lined grill (broiler) pan under a preheated grill (broiler) for about 6 minutes, turning once and basting often with the marinade, until cooked. Transfer to a warmed serving platter. Garnish with coriander (cilantro) and serve with the dipping sauce.

FRESH FISH

You can substitute firm fish for the prawns (shrimp) in this recipe if you wish. Fresh tuna or monkfish would be ideal. Just make sure that the fish is cooked through before you serve it.

STEP 1

STEP 2

STEP 3

STEP 4

KING PRAWNS (JUMBO SHRIMP) IN RED CURRY SAUCE

For something very quick and simple that sets your tastebuds alight, try this inspired dish of prawns (shrimp) in a wonderfully spicy sauce.

SERVES 4

1 tbsp vegetable oil
6 spring onions (scallions), trimmed and sliced
1 stalk lemon grass
1 cm/¹/₂ inch piece fresh ginger root
250 ml/8 fl oz/1 cup coconut milk
2 tbsp Red Curry Paste (see page 102)
1 tbsp fish sauce
500 g/1 lb/3 cups uncooked king prawns (jumbo shrimp)
1 tbsp chopped fresh coriander (cilantro)
fresh chillies, to garnish

1 Heat the vegetable oil in a wok or large frying pan (skillet) and fry the spring onions (scallions) gently for about 2 minutes until softened.

2 Bruise the stalk of lemon grass using a meat mallet or rolling pin. Peel and finely grate the piece of fresh ginger root.

3 Add the bruised lemon grass and grated ginger root to the wok or frying pan (skillet) with the coconut milk, red curry paste and fish sauce. Heat until almost boiling.

4 Peel the prawns (shrimp), leaving the tails intact. Remove the black vein running down the back of each prawn (shrimp). Add the prawns (shrimp) to the wok or frying pan (skillet) with the chopped coriander (cilantro) and cook gently for 5 minutes.

5 Serve the prawns (shrimp) with the sauce, garnished with fresh chillies.

VARIATIONS

Try this recipe using green curry paste instead of red. You can make your own (see page 104) or buy it already prepared from many supermarkets – look for it in the Oriental foods section.

Use 3 shallots or ¹/₂ small onion instead of the spring onions (scallions), if you prefer.

STEP 1

STEP 2

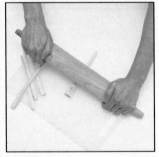

STEP 3

STEP 4

KAFFIR LIME MUSSELS WITH LEMON GRASS

Give fresh mussels a Far Eastern flavour by using some Kaffir lime leaves, garlic and lemon grass in the stock used for steaming them.

SERVES 4

750 g/ 1½ lb live mussels
1 tbsp sesame oil
3 shallots, chopped finely
2 garlic cloves, chopped finely
1 stalk lemon grass
2 Kaffir lime leaves
2 tbsp chopped fresh coriander (cilantro)
finely grated rind of 1 lime
2 tbsp lime juice
300 ml/½ pint/ 1¼ cups hot vegetable stock
crusty bread, to serve

TO GARNISH:
fresh coriander (cilantro) sprigs
lime wedges

1 Using a small sharp knife, scrape the beards off the mussels under cold running water. Scrub them well, discarding any that are damaged or remain open when tapped. Keep rinsing until there is no trace of sand.

2 Heat the sesame oil in a large saucepan and fry the shallots and garlic gently for about 2 minutes until softened.

3 Bruise the lemon grass, using a meat mallet or rolling pin.

4 Add the lemon grass to the saucepan with the Kaffir lime leaves, coriander (cilantro), lime rind and juice, mussels and stock. Put the lid on the saucepan and cook over a medium heat so that the mussels steam for 3–5 minutes. Shake the saucepan from time to time.

5 Check that the mussels have opened and discard any that remain shut. Lift them out into 4 warmed soup plates. Boil the remaining liquid rapidly so that it reduces slightly. Remove the lemon grass and Kaffir lime leaves, then pour the liquid over the mussels.

6 Garnish with the fresh coriander (cilantro) and lime wedges, and serve at once with chunks of crusty bread to soak up the juices.

MUSSELS

Mussels are now farmed, so they should be available from good fishmongers throughout the year.

STEP 1

STEP 2

STEP 3

STEP 4

SHRIMP ROLLS

This variation of a spring roll is made with shrimps, stir-fried with shallots, carrot, cucumber, bamboo shoots and rice.

SERVES 4

2 tbsp vegetable oil
3 shallots, chopped very finely
1 carrot, cut into matchstick pieces
7 cm/ 3 inch piece cucumber, cut into
    matchstick pieces
60 g/2 oz/¹/₂ cup bamboo shoots, drained
    and shredded finely
125 g/4 oz/¹/₂ cup peeled shrimps (small
    shrimp)
90 g/ 3 oz/¹/₂ cup cooked long-grain rice
1 tbsp fish sauce or light soy sauce
1 tsp sugar
2 tsp cornflour (cornstarch), blended in
    2 tbsp cold water
8 × 25 cm/ 10 inch spring roll wrappers
oil for deep-frying
salt and pepper
Thai plum sauce, to serve

TO GARNISH:
spring onion (scallion) brushes (page 172)
fresh coriander (cilantro) sprigs

1 Heat the oil in a wok or frying pan (skillet) and add the shallots, carrot, cucumber and bamboo shoots. Stir-fry briskly for 2–3 minutes. Add the shrimps and cooked rice, and cook for a further 2 minutes. Season.

2 Mix together the fish sauce or soy sauce, sugar and blended cornflour (cornstarch). Add to the stir-fry and cook, stirring constantly, for about 1 minute, until thickened. Leave to cool slightly.

3 Place spoonfuls of the shrimp and vegetable mixture on the spring roll wrappers. Dampen the edges and roll them up to enclose the filling completely.

4 Heat the oil for deep-frying and fry the spring rolls until crisp and golden brown. Drain on paper towels.

5 Serve the shrimp rolls garnished with spring onion (scallion) brushes and fresh coriander (cilantro) and accompanied by the plum sauce.

TIPS

Keep the unfilled spring roll wrappers covered with a clean, damp cloth as you work to prevent them from drying out. Follow the wrapping instructions carefully so that the filling is properly enclosed.

You need 30 g/1 oz/2 tablespoons long-grain rice to give 90 g/3 oz/¹/₂ cup cooked rice.

THAI-STYLE SEAFOOD OMELETTE

This delicious omelette is filled with a mixture of fresh vegetables,
sliced squid and prawns (shrimp).

STEP 1

SERVES 4

4 eggs
3 tbsp milk
1 tbsp fish sauce or light soy sauce
1 tbsp sesame oil
3 shallots, sliced finely
1 small red (bell) pepper, cored, deseeded and
*   sliced very finely*
1 small leek, trimmed and cut into
*   matchstick pieces*
125 g/4 oz squid rings
125 g/4 oz/²⁄₃ cup cooked peeled prawns
*   (shrimp)*
1 tbsp chopped fresh basil
15 g/¹⁄₂ oz/1 tbsp butter
salt and pepper
sprigs of fresh basil, to garnish

1 Beat the eggs, milk and fish sauce
or soy sauce together.

2 Heat the sesame oil in a wok or
large frying pan (skillet) and add all
the vegetables. Stir-fry briskly for 2–3
minutes.

3 Add the squid, prawns (shrimp)
and chopped basil to the wok or
frying pan (skillet). Stir-fry for a further
2–3 minutes until the squid looks
opaque. Season with salt and pepper.

Transfer to a warmed plate and keep
warm.

4 Melt the butter in a large omelette
pan or frying pan (skillet) and add
the beaten egg mixture. Cook over a
medium-high heat until just set.

5 Spoon the vegetable and seafood
mixture in a line down the middle
of the omelette, then fold each side of the
omelette over. Transfer to a warmed
serving dish and cut into 4 portions.
Garnish with sprigs of fresh basil and
serve at once.

STEP 2

STEP 3

VARIATIONS

Chopped, cooked chicken makes a
delicious alternative to the squid.
    Use fresh coriander (cilantro) instead of
the basil for a change.

STEP 5

STEP 2

STEP 3

STEP 4

STEP 5

CRAB-MEAT CAKES

Make these tasty crab-meat cakes, with their flavour of Thailand, to serve as a snack or starter, or as an accompaniment to a main meal.

SERVES 4
OVEN: 180°C/350°/GAS MARK 4

90 g/ 3 oz/generous 1 cup long-grain rice
1 tbsp sesame oil
1 small onion, chopped finely
1 large garlic clove, crushed
2 tbsp chopped fresh coriander (cilantro)
200 g/ 7 oz canned crab meat, drained
1 tbsp fish sauce or light soy sauce
250 ml/ 8 fl oz/ 1 cup coconut milk
2 eggs
4 tbsp vegetable oil
salt and pepper
sliced spring onions (scallions), to garnish

1 Cook the rice in plenty of boiling, lightly salted water for about 12 minutes until just tender. Rinse with cold water and drain well.

2 Heat the sesame oil in a small frying pan (skillet) and fry the onion and garlic gently for about 5 minutes until softened and golden brown.

3 In a large bowl, mix together the rice, onion, garlic, coriander (cilantro), crab meat, fish sauce or soy sauce and coconut milk. Season with salt and pepper. Beat the eggs together and add to the mixture.

4 Divide the mixture between 8 greased ramekin dishes or ovenproof teacups and place them in a baking dish or roasting tin (pan) with enough warm water to come halfway up their sides. Place in the preheated oven for about 25 minutes until set. Leave to cool.

5 Turn the crab cakes out of the ramekin dishes or teacups. Heat the vegetable oil in a wok or frying pan (skillet) and fry the crab cakes in the oil until golden brown. Drain on paper towels and serve at once, garnished with sliced spring onions (scallions).

PREPARING AHEAD

If you want, you can prepare these crab cakes up to the point where they have been baked. Cool them, then cover and chill, ready for frying when needed.

STEP 1

STEP 2

STEP 3

STEP 4

SHRIMP & SWEETCORN PATTIES

Chopped shrimps and sweetcorn are combined in a light batter, which is dropped in spoonfuls into hot fat to make these tasty patties.

SERVES 4

125 g/4 oz/1 cup plain (all-purpose) flour
1¹/₂ tsp baking powder
¹/₂ tsp salt
2 eggs
about 250 ml/8 fl oz/1 cup cold water
1 garlic clove, chopped very finely
3 spring onions (scallions), trimmed and
    chopped very finely
250 g/8 oz/1 cup peeled shrimps (small
    shrimp), chopped
125 g/4 oz/¹/₂ cup canned sweetcorn,
    drained
vegetable oil for frying
pepper

TO GARNISH:
spring onion (scallion) brushes
lime slices
1 chilli flower (see page 206)

1 Sift the flour, baking powder and salt into a large bowl. Add the eggs and half the water. Use a whisk to beat the mixture together to make a smooth batter, adding extra water to give the consistency of double (heavy) cream.

2 Add the garlic and spring onions (scallions) to the batter. Cover and set aside for about 30 minutes.

3 Stir the shrimps and sweetcorn into the batter, mixing well. Season with pepper.

4 Heat 2–3 tablespoons of vegetable oil in a frying pan (skillet). Drop tablespoonfuls of the batter into the pan and cook over a medium heat until bubbles rise and the surface just sets. Flip the patties over and cook the other side until golden brown. Drain on paper towels.

5 Cook the remaining batter in the same way, adding more vegetable oil to the frying pan (skillet) as required.

6 Garnish with a spring onion (scallion) brush, lime slices and a chilli flower and serve at once.

SPRING ONION (SCALLION) BRUSHES

Make a spring onion (scallion) brush by trimming off the tips of the leaves and making several fine cuts from the leaf tips to the top of the bulb. Place in iced water to make the leaves curl.

CHAPTER TWELVE

Poultry

Chicken is a very popular choice for Thai recipes, as its versatile flavour marries so well with other ingredients. It is inexpensive too, which is a bonus. Other poultry, such as duck, is also used, though less frequently as it tends to be more expensive; it is often saved for special occasions.

In most recipes the meat is shredded, chopped or finely minced (ground), so that it combines well with other ingredients and also cooks quickly – especially important for stir-fries and grilled (broiled) or barbecued dishes. Try Sesame Skewered Chicken with Ginger Baste, where the chicken is marinated in a delicious spicy mixture, then threaded on to wooden satay sticks and cooked until golden. And savour the lively flavours in Lime & Coriander (Cilantro) Chicken Fried Rice – if you enjoy it as a side dish, try it as a main course another time.

If you are planning a meal for a large number of guests, make sure that you get the preparations well in hand before their arrival. It's a good idea to measure and assemble all the ingredients that go in any one dish on a large plate, so that you are ready to proceed with the cooking when the time is right. And because Thai cooking is so quick, you'll have time to enjoy the company of your guests!

Opposite: *An exotic Thai temple is reflected in the waters at Mae Hong Son.*

STEP 1

STEP 2

STEP 3

STEP 4

THAI CHICKEN SPRING ROLLS

A cucumber dipping sauce tastes perfect with these delicious spring rolls, filled with chicken and fresh, crunchy vegetables.

SERVES 4

2 tbsp vegetable oil
4 spring onions (scallions), trimmed and
 sliced very finely
1 carrot, cut into matchstick pieces
1 small green or red (bell) pepper, cored,
 deseeded and sliced finely
60 g/2 oz/²/₃ cup button mushrooms, sliced
60 g/2 oz/1 cup bean-sprouts
175 g/6 oz/1 cup cooked chicken, shredded
1 tbsp light soy sauce
1 tsp sugar
2 tsp cornflour (cornstarch), blended in 2
 tbsp cold water
12 × 20 cm/8 inch spring roll wrappers
oil for deep-frying
salt and pepper
spring onion (scallion) brushes, to garnish
 (see page 172)

SAUCE:
50 ml/2 fl oz/¹/₄ cup light malt vinegar
2 tbsp water
60 g/2 oz/¹/₄ cup light muscovado sugar
¹/₂ tsp salt
5 cm/2 inch piece cucumber, peeled and
 chopped finely
4 spring onions (scallions), trimmed and
 sliced finely
1 small red or green chilli, deseeded and
 chopped very finely

1 Heat the oil in a wok or frying pan (skillet) and add the spring onions (scallions), carrot and (bell) pepper. Stir-fry for 2–3 minutes. Add the mushrooms, bean-sprouts and chicken and cook for a further 2 minutes. Season to taste.

2 Mix together the soy sauce, sugar and blended cornflour (cornstarch). Add to the stir-fry and cook, stirring continuously for about 1 minute until thickened. Leave to cool slightly.

3 Place spoonfuls of the chicken and vegetable mixture on the spring roll wrappers. Dampen the edges and roll them up to enclose the filling completely.

4 To make the dipping sauce, heat the vinegar, water, sugar and salt in a saucepan. Boil for 1 minute. Mix the cucumber, spring onions (scallions) and chilli in a small serving bowl and pour over the vinegar mixture. Leave to cool.

5 Heat the oil and fry the rolls until crisp and golden brown. Drain on paper towels, then serve, garnished with spring onion (scallion) brushes and accompanied by the cucumber dipping sauce.

STEP 1

STEP 2

STEP 3

STEP 4

SESAME SKEWERED CHICKEN WITH GINGER BASTE

Chunks of chicken breast are marinated in a mixture of lime juice, garlic, sesame oil and fresh ginger to give them a great flavour.

SERVES 4

4 wooden satay sticks, soaked in warm water
500 g / 1 lb boneless chicken breasts
fresh mint sprigs, to garnish

MARINADE:
1 garlic clove, crushed
1 shallot, chopped very finely
2 tbsp sesame oil
1 tbsp fish sauce or light soy sauce
finely grated rind of 1 lime or ¹/₂ lemon
2 tbsp lime juice or lemon juice
1 tsp sesame seeds
2 tsp finely grated fresh ginger root
2 tsp chopped fresh mint
salt and pepper

1 To make the marinade, put the garlic, shallot, sesame oil, fish sauce or soy sauce, lime or lemon rind and juice, sesame seeds, ginger and chopped mint into a large non-metallic bowl. Season with a little salt and pepper.

2 Remove the skin from the chicken breasts and cut the flesh into chunks. Add them to the marinade, stirring to coat them in the mixture. Cover and chill for at least 2 hours so that the flavours are absorbed.

3 Thread the chicken on to wooden satay sticks. Place them on the rack of a grill (broiler) pan and baste with the marinade.

4 Place the kebabs under a preheated grill (broiler) for 8–10 minutes. Turn them frequently, basting them with the remaining marinade.

5 Serve at once, garnished with sprigs of fresh mint.

VARIATIONS

Pork fillet (tenderloin) or turkey breasts can be used instead of the chicken.
The kebabs taste delicious if dipped into an accompanying bowl of hot chilli sauce.

STEP 1

STEP 2

STEP 3

STEP 4

CHICKEN & MUSHROOM WONTONS

These deliciously crispy nibbles make an ideal introduction to a Thai meal. Here they are filled with a chicken and mushroom mixture.

SERVES 4

250 g/8 oz boneless chicken breast, skinned
60 g/2 oz/²/₃ cup mushrooms
1 garlic clove
2 shallots
1 tbsp fish sauce or mushroom ketchup
1 tbsp chopped fresh coriander (cilantro)
2 tbsp vegetable oil
about 50 wonton wrappers
oil for deep-frying
salt and pepper
sliced spring onion (scallion), to garnish
sweet chilli sauce, to serve

1 Put the chicken, mushrooms, garlic, shallots, fish sauce or mushroom ketchup and coriander (cilantro) into a blender or food processor. Blend for 10–15 seconds. Alternatively, chop all the ingredients finely and mix them together well.

2 Heat the vegetable oil in a wok or frying pan (skillet) and add the chicken mixture. Stir-fry for about 8 minutes, breaking up the mixture as it cooks, until it browns. Transfer to a bowl and leave to cool for 10–15 minutes.

3 Place the wonton wrappers on a clean, damp tea towel (dish cloth).

Layering 2 wrappers together at a time, place teaspoonfuls of the chicken mixture into the middle. Dampen the edges with water, then make small pouches, pressing the edges together to seal. Repeat with the remaining wrappers until all the mixture is used.

4 Heat the oil in a wok or deep-fat fryer. Fry the wontons, a few at a time, for 2–3 minutes until golden brown. Lift them from the oil with a perforated spoon and drain on paper towels. Keep warm while frying the remaining wontons.

5 Transfer the wontons to a warmed serving platter and garnish with sliced spring onion (scallion). Serve at once, accompanied by some sweet chilli sauce.

VARIATIONS

Use 125 g/4 oz/¹/₂ cup of peeled prawns (shrimp) mixed with 125 g/4 oz lean minced (ground) pork to make a different variety, omitting the mushrooms.

If wonton wrappers are unavailable, use sheets of filo pastry cut to size.

DUCKLING & RADISH SALAD

Juicy duckling breasts are coated with sesame seeds, then cooked, thinly sliced and served with a crisp salad.

STEP 1

STEP 2

STEP 3

STEP 4

SERVES 4

350 g/12 oz boneless duckling breasts,
   skinned
2 tbsp plain (all-purpose) flour
1 egg
2 tbsp water
2 tbsp sesame seeds
3 tbsp sesame oil
1/2 head Chinese leaves, shredded
3 celery sticks, sliced finely
8 radishes, trimmed and halved
salt and pepper
fresh basil leaves, to garnish

DRESSING:
finely grated rind of 1 lime
2 tbsp lime juice
2 tbsp olive oil
1 tbsp light soy sauce
1 tbsp chopped fresh basil

1 Put each duckling breast between sheets of greaseproof paper (baking parchment) or clingfilm (plastic wrap). Use a meat mallet or rolling pin to beat them out and flatten them slightly.

2 Sprinkle the flour on to a large plate and season with salt and pepper. Beat the egg and water together in a shallow bowl, then sprinkle the sesame seeds on to a separate plate. Dip the duckling breasts first into the seasoned flour, then into the egg mixture and finally into the sesame seeds.

3 Heat the sesame oil in a wok or frying pan (skillet) and fry the duckling breasts over a medium heat for about 8 minutes, turning once. Insert a sharp knife into the thickest part – the juices should run clear. Lift them out and drain on paper towels.

4 To make the dressing for the salad, whisk together the lime rind and juice, olive oil, soy sauce and chopped basil. Season with a little salt and pepper.

5 Arrange the Chinese leaves, celery and radish on a serving plate. Slice the duckling breasts thinly and place on top of the salad. Drizzle with the dressing and garnish with fresh basil leaves. Serve at once.

VARIATIONS

Use fresh coriander (cilantro) or mint as an alternative to basil.
   Either chicken or turkey breasts would make excellent alternatives to duckling.

STEP 1

STEP 2

STEP 3

STEP 4

LIME & CORIANDER (CILANTRO) CHICKEN FRIED RICE

Lime rind and juice is combined with chopped fresh coriander (cilantro) to give this fried rice recipe a very lively flavour.

SERVES 4

250 g/ 8 oz/ generous 1 cup long-grain rice
4 tbsp vegetable oil
2 garlic cloves, chopped finely
1 small green chilli, deseeded and chopped
    finely
5 shallots, sliced finely
1 tbsp Green Curry Paste (see page 104)
1 yellow or green (bell) pepper, cored,
    deseeded and chopped
2 celery sticks, sliced finely
250 g/ 8 oz/ 1½ cups cooked chicken,
    chopped
2 tbsp light soy sauce
finely grated rind of 1 lime
2 tbsp lime juice
1 tbsp chopped fresh coriander (cilantro)
30 g/ 1 oz/¼ cup unsalted peanuts, toasted

TO GARNISH:
fresh coriander (cilantro)
finely sliced shallots
lime slices

1 Cook the rice in plenty of boiling, lightly salted water for about 12 minutes until tender. Drain, rinse with cold water and drain thoroughly.

2 Heat the oil in a wok or large frying pan (skillet) and add the garlic. Fry gently for 2 minutes until golden. Add the chilli and shallots, and cook, stirring, for a further 3–4 minutes.

3 Add the curry paste to the wok or frying pan (skillet) and fry for 1 minute, then add the yellow or green (bell) pepper and celery. Stir-fry briskly for 2 minutes.

4 Tip the cooked rice into the wok or frying pan (skillet) and add the chicken, soy sauce, lime rind and juice and chopped coriander (cilantro). Stir-fry over a medium-high heat for 4–5 minutes until the rice is hot.

5 Serve sprinkled with the peanuts and garnished with sprigs of fresh coriander (cilantro), sliced shallots and lime slices.

TIPS

If you don't have a lime handy, but you do have a lemon, use that instead – about half the juice will be enough.

The rice is best if it is cooked the day before. Cover it and keep it chilled until you need it.

CHAPTER THIRTEEN

Beef & Pork

In Thai cookery meat is generally used for special occasions only, to mark a particular event with a celebration or a feast. Thailand is more of a seafood-eating nation than a meat-eating one, so meat is mainly used in small amounts to add flavour and variety to dishes, and is combined with lots of other ingredients to make it go further. Another factor is that in Thailand meat can be expensive, so it is used sparingly.

In this chapter you will find some delicious ideas, from the widely known Pork Satay with a simple-to-make spicy peanut sauce, to the more unusual 'Fat Horses' – a fascinating recipe for a mixture of minced (ground) pork, chicken and prawns (shrimp) combined with lots of exciting flavourings cooked together to make an enticing side dish. And if you've ever tried Pork & Prawn (Shrimp) Sesame Toasts in a Thai restaurant, you will be pleased to find this delicious recipe explained here.

The principle of using a little meat with plenty of vegetables, rice and noodles is very sound, nutritionally speaking. It means that our intake of important nutrients – such as vitamins, minerals and complex carbohydrates – is kept high, while our fat intake remains low. Fresh vegetables provide lots of fibre too – essential for keeping our bodies fit from the inside!

Opposite: *Kata Noi beach at dusk.*

STEP 1

STEP 2

STEP 3

STEP 4

PORK & PRAWN (SHRIMP) SESAME TOASTS

This classic Thai snack is a great nibble for serving at parties – but be sure to make plenty!

SERVES 4

250 g/8 oz lean pork
250 g/8 oz/²/₃ cup uncooked peeled prawns
    (shrimp), deveined
4 spring onions (scallions), trimmed
1 garlic clove, crushed
1 tbsp chopped fresh coriander (cilantro)
    leaves and stems
1 tbsp fish sauce
1 egg
8–10 slices thick-cut white bread
3 tbsp sesame seeds
150 ml/¹/₄ pint/²/₃ cup vegetable oil
salt and pepper

TO GARNISH:
sprigs of fresh coriander (cilantro)
red (bell) pepper, sliced finely

1 Put the pork, prawns (shrimp), spring onions (scallions), garlic, coriander (cilantro), fish sauce, egg and seasoning into a food processor or blender. Process for a few seconds to chop the ingredients finely. Transfer the mixture to a bowl. Alternatively, chop the pork, prawns (shrimp) and spring onions (scallions) very finely, and mix with the garlic, coriander (cilantro), fish sauce, beaten egg and seasoning until well combined.

2 Spread the pork and prawn (shrimp) mixture thickly over the bread so that it reaches right up to the edges. Cut off the crusts and slice each piece of bread into 4 squares or triangles.

3 Sprinkle the topping liberally with sesame seeds.

4 Heat the oil in a wok or frying pan (skillet). Fry a few pieces of the bread, topping side down first so that it sets the egg, for about 2 minutes or until golden brown. Turn the pieces over to cook on the other side, about 1 minute.

5 Drain the pork and prawn (shrimp) toasts and place them on paper towels. Fry the remaining pieces in batches until they are all cooked.

6 Serve garnished with sprigs of fresh coriander (cilantro) and strips of red (bell) pepper.

PRAWNS (SHRIMP)

If you can't find any uncooked prawns (shrimp), use cooked ones instead. If using frozen prawns (shrimp), be sure to defrost them first and dry them with paper towels.

STEP 1

STEP 2

STEP 3

STEP 4

PORK SATAY

Small pieces of tender pork are skewered on bamboo satay sticks, grilled (broiled) or barbecued, then served with a delicious peanut sauce.

SERVES 4

8 bamboo satay sticks, soaked in warm
   water
500 g/ 1 lb pork fillet (tenderloin)

SAUCE:
125 g/4oz/1 cup unsalted peanuts
2 tsp hot chilli sauce
180 ml/6 fl oz/³/₄ cup coconut milk
2 tbsp soy sauce
1 tbsp ground coriander
pinch ground turmeric
1 tbsp dark muscovado sugar
salt

TO GARNISH:
fresh flat-leaf parsley or coriander (cilantro)
cucumber leaves
red chillies

1 To make the sauce, scatter the peanuts on a baking sheet (cookie sheet) and toast under a preheated grill (broiler) until golden brown, turning them once or twice. Leave to cool, then grind them in a food processor, blender or food mill. Alternatively, chop them very finely.

2 Put the ground peanuts into a small saucepan with all the

remaining sauce ingredients. Heat gently, stirring constantly. Reduce the heat to very low and cook gently for 5 minutes.

3 Meanwhile, trim any fat from the pork. Cut the pork into small cubes and thread it on to the bamboo satay sticks. Place the kebabs on a rack covered with foil in a grill (broiler) pan.

4 Put half the peanut sauce into a small serving bowl. Brush the skewered pork with the remaining satay sauce and place under a preheated grill (broiler) for about 10 minutes, turning and basting frequently, until cooked.

5 Serve the pork with the reserved peanut sauce and garnish with flat-leaf parsley or coriander (cilantro) leaves, cucumber leaves and red chillies.

CUCUMBER LEAVES

To make cucumber leaves, slice a thick chunk from the side of a cucumber, and cut to shape. Cut grooves in the cucumber flesh in the shape of leaf veins.

FAT HORSES

The curious name for this traditional steamed or baked Thai dish conjures up quite a picture! It is a mixture of minced (ground) pork, chicken and crab meat, flavoured with coconut milk, fish sauce and fresh coriander (cilantro).

STEP 1

STEP 2

STEP 3

STEP 4

SERVES 6

30 g/1 oz/2 tbsp creamed coconut
125 g/4 oz lean pork
125 g/4 oz chicken breast, skin removed
125 g/4 oz/¹/₂ cup canned crab meat, drained
2 eggs
2 garlic cloves, crushed
4 spring onions (scallions), trimmed and chopped
1 tbsp fish sauce
1 tbsp chopped fresh coriander (cilantro) leaves and stems
1 tbsp dark muscovado sugar
salt and pepper

TO GARNISH:
finely sliced white radish (mooli) or turnip
chives
red chilli
fresh coriander (cilantro) sprigs

1 Put the coconut into a bowl and pour over 3 tablespoons of hot water. Stir to dissolve the coconut.

2 Put the pork, chicken and crab meat into a food processor or blender and process for 10–15 seconds until minced (ground), or chop them finely by hand and put in a mixing bowl.

3 Add the coconut mixture to the food processor or blender with the eggs, garlic, spring onions (scallions), fish sauce, coriander (cilantro) and sugar. Season with salt and pepper and process for a few more seconds. Alternatively, mix these ingredients into the chopped pork, chicken and crab meat.

4 Grease 6 ramekin dishes with a little butter. Spoon in the minced (ground) mixture, levelling the surface. Place them in a steamer, then set it over a pan of gently boiling water. Cook for about 30 minutes until set.

5 Lift out the dishes and leave to cool for a few minutes. Run a knife around the edge of each dish, then invert it on to warmed plates. Serve garnished with finely sliced white radish (mooli) or turnip, chives, red chilli and sprigs of fresh coriander (cilantro).

BAKING

You can bake the mixture in a preheated oven at 180°C/350°F/Gas Mark 4 for 30 minutes if preferred, placing the dishes in a roasting tin (pan), with enough warm water to come halfway up their sides.

MEATBALLS IN SPICY PEANUT SAUCE

Choose very lean minced (ground) beef to make these meatballs – or better still, buy some lean beef and mince (grind) it yourself.

STEP 1

SERVES 4

500 g/1 lb lean minced (ground) beef
2 tsp finely grated fresh ginger root
1 small red chilli, deseeded and chopped
    finely
1 tbsp chopped fresh basil or coriander
    (cilantro)
1 tbsp sesame oil
1 tbsp vegetable oil
salt and pepper

SAUCE:
2 tbsp Red Curry Paste (see page 102)
300 ml/¹/₂ pint/1¹/₄ cups coconut milk
125 g/4 oz/1 cup ground peanuts
1 tbsp fish sauce

TO GARNISH:
chopped fresh basil
fresh basil or coriander (cilantro) sprigs

1 Put the beef, ginger, chilli and basil or coriander (cilantro) into a food processor or blender. Add ¹/₂ teaspoon of salt and plenty of pepper. Process for 10–15 seconds until finely chopped. Alternatively, chop the ingredients finely and mix together.

2 Form the beef mixture into about 12 balls. Heat the sesame oil and vegetable oil in a wok or frying pan (skillet) and fry the meatballs over a medium-high heat for about 10 minutes until well browned on all sides. Lift them out and drain on paper towels.

STEP 2

3 To make the sauce, stir-fry the red curry paste in the wok or frying pan (skillet) for 1 minute. Add the coconut milk, peanuts and fish sauce. Heat, stirring, until just simmering.

4 Return the meatballs to the wok or frying pan (skillet) and cook gently in the sauce for 10–15 minutes. If the sauce begins to get too thick, add a little extra coconut milk or water. Season with a little salt and pepper, if needed.

STEP 3

5 Serve garnished with chopped fresh basil and sprigs of fresh basil or coriander (cilantro).

ALTERNATIVE

Minced (ground) lamb makes a delicious alternative to beef. If you do use lamb, however, substitute ground almonds for the peanuts and fresh mint for the basil.

STEP 4

STEP 1

STEP 2

STEP 3

STEP 4

ROAST RED PORK

Pork fillet (tenderloin) is given a marvellous flavour and distinctive red colour in this excellent recipe.

SERVES 4
OVEN: 220°C/350°F/GAS MARK 7

750 g/1¹/₂ lb pork fillet (tenderloin)
1 tsp red food colouring
4 garlic cloves, crushed
1 tsp Chinese five-spice powder
1 tbsp light soy sauce
1 tbsp fish sauce
1 tbsp dry sherry
1 tbsp dark muscovado sugar
1 tbsp sesame oil
1 tbsp finely grated fresh ginger root

TO GARNISH:
lettuce
spring onions (scallions), sliced finely

1 Rinse the pork fillet (tenderloin) and trim off any fat. Place in a large clear plastic food bag or freezer bag and add the red food colouring. Roll the pork around in the bag to coat it in the colouring.

2 Mix all the remaining ingredients together in a bowl.

3 Add the mixture to the pork in the plastic bag. Secure the opening and chill overnight, or for at least 12 hours, turning the bag over occasionally.

4 Place the pork on a rack over a roasting tin (pan) and cook in the preheated oven for 15 minutes. Remove from the oven and baste with the remaining marinade.

5 Reduce the oven temperature to 180°C/350°F/Gas Mark 4 and return the pork to the oven to roast for a further 25 minutes, basting occasionally with any remaining marinade. Leave to cool for at least 10 minutes before slicing.

6 Slice thinly, arrange on a serving platter and garnish with lettuce and finely sliced spring onions (scallions).

PORK

Putting the pork in a plastic bag helps to prevent your hands from turning red from the food colouring.

Roast red pork makes an excellent addition to stir-fries and fried rice and noodle dishes.

STEP 1

STEP 2

STEP 3

STEP 4

STIR-FRIED PORK & CABBAGE

Rustle up this quick-to-cook side dish in a matter of moments.
Assemble all your ingredients first, then everything is ready to hand
as you start to stir-fry.

SERVES 4

375 g / 12 oz pork fillet (tenderloin)
8 spring onions (scallions), trimmed
1/2 small white cabbage
1/2 cucumber
2 tsp finely grated fresh ginger root
1 tbsp fish sauce or light soy sauce
2 tbsp dry sherry
2 tbsp water
2 tsp cornflour (cornstarch)
1 tbsp chopped fresh mint or coriander
  (cilantro)
2 tbsp sesame oil
salt and pepper

TO GARNISH:
fresh mint or coriander (cilantro) sprigs
1 chilli flower (see page 206)

1 Slice the pork very thinly. Shred the spring onions (scallions) and cabbage, and cut the cucumber into matchstick strips.

2 Mix together the ginger, fish sauce or soy sauce, sherry, water, cornflour (cornstarch) and chopped mint or coriander (cilantro) until blended.

3 Heat the sesame oil in a wok or large frying pan (skillet) and add

the pork. Stir-fry briskly over a high heat for 4–5 minutes until browned.

4 Add the spring onions (scallions), cabbage and cucumber and stir-fry for a further 2 minutes. Add the blended cornflour (cornstarch) mixture and continue to cook for about 1 minute until the pork and vegetables are coated with the mixture and it has thickened slightly. Season to taste with salt and pepper.

5 Transfer the stir-fry to a warmed dish and serve at once, garnished with sprigs of fresh mint or coriander (cilantro) and a chilli flower.

ROAST RED PORK

Roast Red Pork is excellent used in this stir-fry, as it adds both extra colour and flavour. See the recipe on page 196.

STEP 1

STEP 2

STEP 3

STEP 4

THAI STUFFED COURGETTES (ZUCCHINI)

Hollow out some courgettes (zucchini), fill them with a spicy beef mixture and bake them in the oven for a delicious side dish.

SERVES 4
OVEN: 190°C/375°F/GAS MARK 5

8 medium courgettes (zucchini)
1 tbsp sesame or vegetable oil
1 garlic clove, crushed
2 shallots, chopped finely
1 small red chilli, deseeded and chopped
   finely
250 g/8 oz lean minced (ground) beef
1 tbsp fish sauce or mushroom ketchup
1 tbsp chopped fresh coriander (cilantro) or
   basil
2 tsp cornflour (cornstarch), blended with a
   little cold water
90 g/3 oz /1½ cup cooked long-grain rice
salt and pepper

TO GARNISH:
fresh coriander (cilantro) or basil sprigs
carrot slices

1 Slice the courgettes (zucchini) in half horizontally and scoop out a channel down the middle, discarding all the seeds. Sprinkle with salt and set aside for 15 minutes.

2 Heat the oil in a wok or frying pan (skillet) and add the garlic, shallots and chilli. Stir-fry for 2 minutes, until golden. Add the minced (ground) beef and stir-fry briskly for about 5 minutes. Stir in the fish sauce or mushroom ketchup, the chopped coriander (cilantro) or basil and the blended cornflour (cornstarch) and cook for 2 minutes, stirring until thickened. Season with salt and pepper, then remove from the heat.

3 Rinse the courgettes (zucchini) in cold water and arrange them in a greased shallow ovenproof dish, cut side uppermost. Mix the cooked rice into the minced (ground) beef, then use this mixture to stuff the courgettes (zucchini).

4 Cover with foil and bake in the preheated oven for 20–25 minutes, removing the foil for the last 5 minutes of cooking time. Serve at once, garnished with sprigs of fresh coriander (cilantro) or basil, and carrot slices.

VARIATIONS

Minced (ground) pork or chicken can be used instead of beef.
   Vary the type of vegetables that you use. Aubergines (eggplants), large mushrooms and extra-large tomatoes all make good alternatives.

CHAPTER FOURTEEN

Vegetables

In all Thai cookery, vegetables are used in abundance to add taste, colour and 'crunch' to an array of different dishes. They feature in many recipes for side dishes and stir-fries, in which they are cooked quickly to retain all their goodness and flavour. Quick cooking is one of the hallmarks of this country's vibrant cuisine, and Thai cooks take care to assemble all their ingredients before they start to cook, so that everything is to hand when things start to sizzle!

Obtaining fresh produce to use in Thai cookery shouldn't present a problem, as there is now such a wide range of fresh vegetables available, and it is easy to adapt and make substitutions that will work equally well. So while it may not always be possible to use the exact ingredient, dishes with a good degree of authenticity can still be achieved. For instance, where bok choy is used in the recipe for Stir-fried Greens, spring cabbage or spinach could be used instead.

Remember that in Thai cookery a few key ingredients can capture the flavour of the country. Coconut milk, fish sauce, fresh coriander (cilantro), lemon grass, Kaffir lime leaves and fresh chillies are all typical ingredients in many dishes from Thailand, and are all becoming more widely available.

Opposite: *A stunning display of colourful and exotic ingredients in a Thai marketplace.*

STEP 1

STEP 2

STEP 3

STEP 4

DEEP-FRIED VEGETABLES WITH SWEET & SOUR SAUCE

Choose a selection of your favourite seasonal vegetables, coat them in a light batter and deep-fry them until crispy to make this delightful dish.

SERVES 4

500 g/1 lb selection fresh vegetables, such as red and green (bell) peppers, courgettes (zucchini), carrots, spring onions (scallions), cauliflower, broccoli and mushrooms
oil for deep-frying

BATTER:
125 g/4 oz/1 cup plain (all-purpose) flour
1/2 tsp salt
1 tsp caster (superfine) sugar
1 tsp baking powder
3 tbsp vegetable oil
200 ml/7 fl oz/scant 1 cup tepid water

SAUCE:
1 tbsp light muscovado sugar
2 tbsp soy sauce
4 tbsp cider vinegar
4 tbsp medium sherry
1 tbsp cornflour (cornstarch)
1 tsp finely grated fresh ginger root

TO GARNISH:
spring onion (scallion) brushes (see page 172)
chopped spring onions (scallions)

1 To make the batter, sift the flour, salt, sugar and baking powder into a large bowl. Add the oil and most of the water. Whisk together to make a smooth batter, adding extra water to give it the consistency of single (light) cream. Chill for 20–30 minutes.

2 To make the sauce, put all the ingredients into a small saucepan. Heat, stirring, until thickened and smooth.

3 Cut all the vegetables into even, bite-sized pieces.

4 Heat the oil in a wok or deep fat fryer. Dip the vegetables into the batter and fry them in the hot oil, a few at a time, for about 2 minutes until golden brown and crispy. Drain on paper towels.

5 Serve the vegetables on a warmed platter, garnished with spring onion (scallion) brushes and chopped spring onions (scallions), accompanied by the sauce.

SESAME SEEDS

Scatter a few sesame seeds over the crispy-fried vegetables just before serving, if you wish.

STEP 1

STEP 2

STEP 3

STEP 4

BAMBOO SHOOTS WITH CUCUMBER

A simple stir-fried side dish of canned bamboo shoots and sliced cucumber is the perfect accompaniment to a Thai main meal.

SERVES 4

¹/₂ cucumber
2 tbsp sesame oil
4 shallots, chopped finely
1 garlic clove, sliced finely
350 g/12 oz canned bamboo shoots, drained
1 tbsp dry sherry
1 tbsp soy sauce
2 tsp cornflour (cornstarch)
1 tsp sesame seeds
salt

TO GARNISH:
2 red chilli flowers
sliced spring onions (scallions)

1 Slice the cucumber thinly and sprinkle with salt. Leave for 10–15 minutes, then rinse with cold water. To make chilli flowers for garnishing, hold the stem of the chilli and cut down its length several times with a sharp knife. Place in a bowl of chilled water and chill so that the 'petals' turn out. Remove the chilli seeds when the 'petals' have opened.

2 Heat the sesame oil in a wok or frying pan (skillet) and add the shallots and garlic. Stir-fry for 2 minutes, until golden.

3 Add the bamboo shoots and cucumber to the wok or frying pan (skillet) and stir-fry for 2–3 minutes.

4 Blend together the sherry, soy sauce and cornflour (cornstarch). Add to the bamboo shoots and cucumber, stirring to combine. Cook for 1–2 minutes to thicken slightly, then add the sesame seeds and stir them through.

5 Transfer the vegetables to a warmed serving dish. Garnish with the chilli flowers and chopped spring onion (scallion). Serve at once.

TIPS

Salting the cucumber before it is stir-fried draws out some of its moisture so that it stays crisp.
   Add some very finely sliced carrot to this dish to add some extra colour, if you like.

STEP 1

STEP 2

STEP 3

STEP 4

SAUTEED GREENS

Eat your greens in this most delicious way – stir-fried so that they retain their colour, crunch and flavour.

SERVES 4

8 spring onions (scallions)
2 celery sticks
125 g/4 oz white radish (mooli)
125 g/4 oz sugar snap peas or mangetout
  (snow peas)
175 g/6 oz Chinese leaves or cabbage
175 g/6 oz bok choy or spinach
2 tbsp vegetable oil
1 tbsp sesame oil
2 garlic cloves, chopped finely
1 tbsp fish sauce
2 tbsp oyster sauce
1 tsp finely grated fresh ginger root
pepper

1 Slice the spring onions (scallions) and celery finely. Cut the white radish (mooli) into matchstick strips. Trim the sugar snap peas or mangetout (snow peas). Shred the Chinese leaves or cabbage and shred the bok choy or spinach.

2 Heat the vegetable oil and sesame oil together in a wok or large frying pan (skillet). Add the garlic and fry for about 1 minute.

3 Add the spring onions (scallions), celery, white radish (mooli) and sugar snap peas or mangetout (snow peas) to the wok or frying pan (skillet) and stir-fry for about 2 minutes.

4 Add the Chinese leaves or cabbage and bok choy or spinach. Stir-fry for 1 minute.

5 Stir the fish sauce and oyster sauce into the vegetables with the grated ginger. Cook for 1 minute. Season with pepper and serve at once.

VARIATIONS

Any variety – and any amount – of fresh vegetables can be used in this dish. Just make sure that harder vegetables, such as carrots, are cut very finely so that they cook quickly.

Use light soy sauce as an alternative to the fish sauce, if you prefer.

SHREDDED VEGETABLE OMELETTE

Cook this large omelette and then slice into four portions to serve as a side dish. If you like, double the quantities and serve it as a main course.

STEP 1

STEP 2

STEP 3

STEP 4

SERVES 4

4 eggs
3 tbsp milk
1 tbsp fish sauce or light soy sauce
1 tbsp sesame oil
1 small red onion, sliced very finely
1 small courgette (zucchini), trimmed and
*   cut into matchstick pieces*
1 small leek, trimmed and cut into
*   matchstick pieces*
1 small carrot, trimmed and cut into
*   matchstick pieces*
5 cm/2 inch piece cucumber, cut into
*   matchstick pieces*
1 tbsp chopped fresh coriander (cilantro)
15 g/¹/₂ oz/1 tbsp butter
salt and pepper

TO GARNISH:
sprigs of fresh basil
celery leaves
4 chilli flowers (see page 206)

1 Beat the eggs, milk and fish sauce or soy sauce together.

2 Heat the sesame oil in a wok or large frying pan (skillet) and add all the vegetables. Stir-fry them briskly for 3–4 minutes, then add the chopped coriander (cilantro). Season with salt and

pepper. Transfer to a warmed plate and keep warm.

3 Melt the butter in a large omelette pan or frying pan (skillet) and add the beaten egg mixture. Cook over a medium-high heat until just set.

4 Tip the vegetable mixture along one side of the omelette, then roll up the omelette. Slice into 4 portions and arrange on a warmed serving plate. Garnish with fresh basil, celery leaves and chilli flowers and serve at once.

VEGETABLES

Work quickly when making the omelette to make sure that the vegetables retain their just-cooked texture and flavour.

Substitute other vegetables for the ones in the recipe as you wish – spring onions (scallions), mangetout (snow peas), small broccoli or cauliflower florets, for example.

PAW-PAW (PAPAYA) SALAD

Choose firm paw-paws – or papayas as they are sometimes called – for this delicious salad.

STEP 1

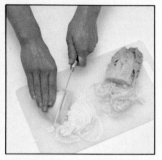

STEP 2

STEP 3

STEP 4

SERVES 4

DRESSING:
4 tbsp olive oil
1 tbsp fish sauce or light soy sauce
2 tbsp lime or lemon juice
1 tbsp dark muscovado sugar
1 tsp finely chopped fresh red or green chilli

SALAD:
1 crisp lettuce
1/4 small white cabbage
2 paw-paws (papayas)
2 tomatoes
30 g/1 oz/1/4 cup roast peanuts, chopped
*   roughly*
4 spring onions (scallions), trimmed and
*   sliced thinly*
basil leaves, to garnish

1 To make the dressing, whisk together the olive oil, fish sauce or soy sauce, lime or lemon juice, sugar and chopped chilli. Set aside, stirring occasionally to dissolve the sugar.

2 Shred the lettuce and cabbage and toss them together. Arrange on a large serving plate.

3 Peel the paw-paws (papayas) and slice them in half. Scoop out the seeds, then slice the flesh thinly. Arrange on top of the shredded lettuce and cabbage.

4 Put the tomatoes into a small bowl and cover them with boiling water. Leave them to stand for 1 minute, then lift them out with a fork and peel them. Remove the seeds and chop the flesh. Arrange them on the salad leaves. Scatter the peanuts and spring onions (scallions) over the top.

5 Whisk the salad dressing to distribute the ingredients and pour over the salad. Garnish with basil leaves and serve at once.

TIPS

Instead of using a fresh chilli in the dressing, use 1/2 teaspoon of dried chilli flakes instead. If you prefer a milder dressing, omit the chilli altogether.

Choose plain, unsalted peanuts and toast them under the grill (broiler) until golden to get the best flavour. Take care not to burn them, as they brown very quickly.

CHAPTER FIFTEEN

Desserts

Few things are more beguiling and enticing than a stunning array of mixed tropical fruits carefully arranged on a platter to round off a meal, and the Thais make this traditional dessert an art form: slices of sunset-coloured mango and paw-paw (papaya) nestle against jewel-like green and black discs of kiwi fruit, wheels of fragrant yellow pineapple and diagonally sliced strips of banana.

Desserts, as we know them, usually only appear at banquets and special festive occasions, although sweet treats can be bought ready-made by street vendors on almost every corner.

When it is time to celebrate the Thais use their wealth of tropical fruits to make superb fruit salads, stuffed pancakes, wontons and baby dumplings. They use rice to make a rich and creamy pudding baked with coconut milk, and purée fruits to make ice creams, parfaits and exotic water ices. The all-time favourite is Thai-style Bananas, sliced and cooked in butter with orange rind, sugar and lime juice, flamed with orange-flavoured liqueur and sprinkled with toasted coconut shreds, all the better for serving with a dollop of coconut-flavoured cream or ice cream. No wonder the Thais save it for best!

Opposite: *A street vendor in Bangkok displays her fruit on banana leaves, often used to wrap and bake fish. The leaves are inedible, but impart a delicate flavour to the cooked fish.*

THAI-STYLE BANANAS

The Thais rarely finish a meal with an elaborate dessert, preferring to eat a selection of tropical fruits. This is one of the exceptions and you can understand why.

SERVES 6

3 tbsp shredded fresh coconut
60 g/ 2 oz/¹/₄ cup unsalted butter
1 tbsp grated ginger root
grated rind of 1 orange
6 bananas
60 g/ 2 oz/¹/₄ cup caster (superfine) sugar
4 tbsp fresh lime juice
6 tbsp orange-flavour liqueur
3 tsp toasted sesame seeds
lime slices, to decorate
ice cream, to serve (optional)

1 Heat a small non-stick frying pan (skillet) until hot. Add the coconut and cook, stirring constantly, for about 1 minute until lightly coloured. Remove from the pan and allow to cool.

2 Heat the butter in a large frying pan (skillet) until it melts. Add the ginger and orange rind and mix well.

3 Peel and slice the bananas lengthways (and halve if they are very large). Place the bananas cut-side down in the butter mixture and cook for 1–2 minutes or until the sauce mixture starts to become sticky. Turn to coat in the sauce.

4 Remove the bananas from the pan and place on heated serving plates. Keep warm.

5 Return the pan to the heat and add the orange liqueur, stirring well to blend. Ignite with a taper, allow the flames to die down, then pour over the bananas.

6 Sprinkle with the coconut and sesame seeds and serve at once, decorated with slices of lime.

> ### VARIATION
>
> For a very special treat try serving with a flavoured ice cream such as coconut, ginger or praline.

STEP 1

STEP 3

STEP 3

STEP 5

MANGO PARFAIT

This is a beautifully soft parfait that can be served straight from the freezer. Serve with crisp dessert biscuits (cookies) or, when time and the waistline allows, with deep-fried, sugar-dusted wontons.

SERVES 4

1 large ripe mango
juice of 1 lime
about 1 tbsp caster (superfine) sugar
3 egg yolks
60 g/2 oz/½ cup icing (confectioners')
    sugar, sifted
150 ml/¼ pint/⅔ cup double (heavy)
    cream
shredded lime rind, to decorate
fried wontons dusted with sugar, to serve
    (optional)

1 Peel the mango and slice the flesh away from the stone. Purée in a food processor or blender with the lime juice and caster (superfine) sugar to taste, until the mixture is smooth.

2 Beat the egg yolks with the icing (confectioners') sugar until the mixture is pale and thick, then fold in the mango purée.

3 Whip the cream until it stands in soft peaks. Fold into the mango mixture with a metal spoon.

4 Pour the mango mixture into 4 freezerproof serving glasses and freeze until firm, about 4–6 hours.

5 Serve the parfaits straight from the freezer (they will be soft enough to scoop) with crisp dessert biscuits (cookies) or warm fried wontons (see instructions below) dusted with sugar.

FRIED WONTONS

Allow about 2 wontons per person. Deep-fry the wonton skins in hot oil for about 30 seconds until crisp and golden. Drain on paper towels, then dust with icing (confectioners') sugar to serve.

BAKED COCONUT RICE PUDDING

A wonderful baked rice pudding cooked with flavoursome coconut milk and a little lime rind. Serve hot or chilled with fresh or stewed fruit.

STEP 1

STEP 2

STEP 3

STEP 3

SERVES 4–6
OVEN: 170°C/325°F/GAS MARK 2

90 g/ 3 oz/scant ⅓ cup short or round-grain
   pudding rice
600 ml/ 1 pint/ 2½ cups coconut milk
300 ml/ ½ pint/ 1¼ cups milk
1 large strip lime rind
60 g/ 2 oz/ ¼ cup caster (superfine) sugar
knob butter
pinch ground star anise (optional)
fresh or stewed fruit, to serve

1 Mix the rice with the coconut milk, milk, lime rind and sugar.

2 Pour the rice mixture into a lightly greased 1.5 litre/2½ pint/6¼ cup shallow ovenproof dish and dot the surface with a little butter. Bake in the oven for about 30 minutes.

3 Remove and discard the strip of lime. Stir the pudding well, add the pinch of ground star anise, if using, return to the oven and cook for a further 1–2 hours or until almost all the milk has been absorbed and a golden brown skin has baked on the top of the pudding. Cover the top of the pudding with foil if it starts to brown too much towards the end of the cooking time.

4 Serve the pudding warm or chilled with fresh or stewed fruit.

COOK'S TIP

As the mixture cools it thickens. If you plan to serve the rice chilled, fold in about 3 tablespoons cream or extra coconut milk before serving to give a thinner consistency.

STEP 1

STEP 2

STEP 2

STEP 5

FRUIT SALAD WITH GINGER SYRUP

This is a very special fruit salad made from the most exotic and colourful fruits that are soaked in a syrup made with fresh ginger and ginger wine.

SERVES 6–8

2.5 cm/1 in ginger root, peeled and chopped
60 g/2 oz/¼ cup caster (superfine) sugar
150 ml/¼ pint/⅔ cup water
grated rind and juice of 1 lime
4 tbsp ginger wine
1 fresh pineapple, peeled, cored and cut into
   bite-sized pieces
2 ripe mangoes, peeled, stoned and diced
4 kiwi fruit, peeled and sliced
1 paw-paw (papaya), peeled, deseeded and
   diced
2 passion-fruit, halved and flesh removed
350 g/12 oz lychees, peeled and stoned
   (pitted)
¼ fresh coconut, grated
60 g/2 oz Cape gooseberries, to decorate
   (optional)
coconut ice cream, to serve (optional)

1 Place the ginger, sugar, water and lime juice in a small pan and bring slowly to the boil. Simmer for 1 minute, remove from the heat and allow the syrup to cool slightly.

2 Pass the sugar syrup through a fine sieve (strainer), then add the ginger wine and mix well. Allow to cool completely.

3 Place the prepared pineapple, mango, kiwi, paw-paw (papaya), passion-fruit and lychees in a serving bowl. Add the cold syrup and mix well. Cover and chill for 2–4 hours.

4 Just before serving, add half of the grated coconut to the salad and mix well. Sprinkle the remainder on the top of the fruit salad.

5 If using Cape gooseberries to decorate the fruit salad, peel back each calyx to form a flower. Wipe the berries with a damp cloth, then arrange them around the side of the fruit salad before serving.

PANCAKES POLAMAI

These Thai pancakes are filled with an exotic array of tropical fruits.
Decorate lavishly with tropical flowers or mint sprigs.

SERVES 4

BATTER:
125 g/4 oz/1 cup plain (all-purpose) flour
pinch salt
1 egg
1 egg yolk
300 ml/¹/₂ pint/1¹/₄ cups coconut milk
4 tsp vegetable oil, plus oil for frying

FILLING:
1 banana
1 paw-paw (papaya)
juice of 1 lime
2 passion-fruit
1 mango, peeled, stoned and sliced
4 lychees, stoned and halved
1–2 tbsp honey
flowers or mint sprigs, to decorate

1 To make the batter, sift the flour into a bowl with the salt. Make a well in the centre, add the egg and egg yolk and a little of the coconut milk. Gradually draw the flour into the egg mixture, beating well and gradually adding the remaining coconut milk to make a smooth batter. Add the oil and mix well. Cover and chill for 30 minutes.

2 To make the filling, peel and slice the banana and place in a bowl.

Peel and slice the paw-paw (papaya), remove and discard the seeds then cut into bite-sized chunks. Add to the banana with the lime juice and mix well to coat.

3 Cut the passion-fruit in half and scoop out the flesh and seeds into the fruit bowl. Add the mango, lychees and honey and mix well.

4 To make the pancakes, heat a little oil in a 15 cm/6 inch crêpe pan or frying pan (skillet). Pour in just enough of the pancake batter to cover the base of the pan and tilt so that it spreads thinly and evenly. Cook until the pancake is just set and the underside is lightly browned, turn and briefly cook the other side. Remove from the pan and keep warm. Repeat with the remaining batter to make a total of 8 pancakes.

5 To serve, place a little of the prepared fruit filling along the centre of each pancake and then, using both hands, roll it into a cone shape. Lay seam-side down on warmed serving plates, allowing 2 pancakes per serving.

6 Serve the stuffed pancakes at once, decorated with flowers and mint sprigs, if liked.

STEP 1

STEP 2

STEP 3

STEP 4

COMPLETE THAI COOKING

Thai Cuisine

THAI CUISINE

STYLISH GARNISHES

No Thai meal is complete without beautiful garnishes made from fresh fruit or vegetables. Here are some simple techniques that can add style and flair to your presentation.

Chilli flower Use a long, thin fresh chilli. Carefully make 6 slices in the chilli from almost at the base to the tip all the way round, to make the petals. Chill in cold water for at least 30 minutes until the strips curl into petals.

Tomato rose Use a very sharp paring knife to cut the skin off a tomato in a long strip, starting at the top and working around to the bottom. Roll up the strip, starting very tightly but then rolling more loosely until the roll resembles a full-blown rose.

Onion flower Cut a piece of spring onion (scallion) stem about 7.5 cm/3 inches long. Cut very thin slices from both ends that almost meet in the middle; do not cut all the way through. Chill in cold water for at least 30 minutes until the sections curl into petals.

Welcome to the world of Thai cooking – a cuisine full of colours, flavours and sheer vibrancy, where the natural good taste of the most delicious ingredients is never disguised. Blessed with rich natural resources and a reliable climate, Thai cooks have been able to develop and refine a cuisine that is unique. It is not difficult, however, to spot the influence of near neighbours China and India in Thailand's stir-fries and curries, yet there is always the distinct Thai style with the use of herbs, spices and the ever-present coconut. The result is light, aromatic and zestful food that can also be hot, robust and full-flavoured. Spicy 'heat' is one of the unmistakable characteristics of Thai food, reflecting the fact that more than half a dozen of the world's hottest chillies are indigenous to the country.

The uniqueness of Thai food can be sampled in the light stir-fries which are not thickened with cornflour (cornstarch) as they are in China, curries based on a freshly pounded paste of fresh herbs and spices, rather than the blends of dry flavourings that are used in India, and the liberal use of coconut milk.

Thai cuisine centres around the country's bountiful rice harvests and its rich supplies of green vegetables, herbs, spices and fruit. The thousands of miles of coastline and numerous inland waterways also mean that at least one fish or seafood dish – be it sizzling prawns (shrimp), a spicy fish curry or a baked whole fish wrapped in banana leaves – usually features in every meal. Meat,

including beef, cattle and poultry, also contributes to the varied cuisine, as the country's religious groups impose few of the dietary restrictions which are commonplace in nearby countries.

Meals and menus

When a Thai family or group of friends sit down to enjoy a meal, numerous dishes are served at once, with a large bowl of rice holding pride of place in the centre. Everyone will simply help themselves without being expected to wait until they are served. International hotels in Thailand and Thai restaurants around the world cater for Western conventions by separating soups and appetizers into separate courses, but that is not the traditional Thai style.

A typical family menu may include a clear soup, a steamed dish, a fried dish, a slowly cooked curry, a bowl of sauce for dipping individual portions into and a salad. When a dessert is served it will be a liquid or dry sweet dish, or a beautifully presented platter or carved basket of fresh fruit. Thai salads, elaborate combinations of vegetables and fruit with strips of meat and seafood, are assembled with the intention of achieving a balanced mix of colours, flavours and textures.

Unlike many of their neighbours in South-East Asia, Thais prefer using spoons to using chopsticks, except when eating noodles, so when a meal is served there won't be any serving spoons and all the dishes will be served communally. Everyone will have a plate for rice in front of them. The diners use their own spoons to scoop up a small portion of one the dishes and bring the food back to their plate to eat with the rice before moving on to the next dish. This will continue until everyone has had as much to eat as they want.

The Thai are great snackers and eating between meals is a regular feature of everyday life. Street vendors on almost every corner sell tempting selections of small, often sweet appetizers and other finger foods. These can be anything from fried rice cakes, skewers of barbecued meat with peanut sauce or noodle dishes to thick, juicy slices of exotic fruit.

Abundant rice

Rice is such an important part of Thai culture as well as its cuisine that a host or hostess starts a meal with the refrain *kin-khao*, literally 'eat rice'. Most Thais will eat rice at least once day, and may well have some with every meal. Modern influences are breaking down age-old traditions, but not long ago most Thais would begin the day with rice porridge or a meat and rice soup for breakfast.

Long and short grain rices are staples of the Thai kitchen, and are prepared in a variety of ways – boiling, stir-frying and deep-frying. The bland flavour of simply prepared rice provides the perfect counter-balance to spicier, more flavourful ingredients.

Thai jasmine rice has a lovely aromatic scent and long, slender grains. It is sold in specialist Thai food stores and adds an authentic flavour to any Thai meal.

Short-grain rice is commonly called sticky rice because the grains can be literally squeezed together into a solid mass after it has been cooked. Popular for serving in desserts, sticky rice is also often wrapped in banana leaves and steamed. The short grains are also ground into a fine flour that thickens very liquid dishes and is used for making dumplings, cakes and pastries.

Creamy coloured rice noodles, made from ground rice, are also popular and regularly included in soups and stir-fried and deep-fried dishes. Although they are virtually tasteless, they are appreciated by cooks because they absorb the flavour or any other ingredients they are cooked with. Clever Thai cooks also deep-fry the noodles as an edible garnish for other dishes.

Beautiful presentation

Attractive, inviting presentation of food is just as important to Thai cooks as the balanced flavouring of dishes. Great care is taken not only with the careful selection and preparation of ingredients, but also with the intricate fruit and vegetable carving used to decorate dishes when they are served.

Skilled artisans work calmly and delicately to make the most elaborate carving from almost any fruit and vegetable, including cucumbers, firm carrots and radishes. Almost as if by magic, an accomplished Thai carver can transform a piece of fresh ginger into life-like looking crab, complete with long sharp pinchers. Pineapples and melons are hollowed out with elaborate patterns carved in the skin or peel to make decorative containers for serving from or to make a table centrepiece.

Carrot rolls Use a vegetable peeler to cut very thin strip of carrot, cutting the whole length. Roll up the strips, then spear three with a wooden cocktail stick (toothpick). Chill in cold water for at least 30 minutes. Remove sticks before using.

Deep-fried garlic Thinly slice peeled cloves of garlic. Heat a wok over a high heat, then add vegetable oil and heat until it is 180°C/350°F or until a cube of bread browns in 60 seconds. Add the garlic slices and deep-fry until golden brown and crisp looking. Remove with a deep-frying ladle and drain well on paper towels. Use to garnish rice dishes.

Pineapple basket Use a cleaver of heavy cook's knife to halve a pineapple lengthwise; do not cut off the grey-green leaves at the top. Use a small paring knife to cut out all the flesh. Do not worry if you can not get the flesh to come out in one piece. Cut out any small brown 'eyes'. Remove the core, then finely dice the flesh.

To make an exotic fruit salad to serve in the pineapple basket, mix the pineapple flesh with a selection of other tropical fruit and squeeze over fresh orange juice and lime juice. Gently toss together with your hands, then return the fruit salad to the hollowed-out pineapple. Sprinkle with freshly grated coconut.

1. If you are using a round-bottomed wok, put it on a wok rack so it rests securely.

2. Only half-fill the wok with oil.

3. Use long chopsticks or a long-handled wooden spoon for stirring the food while it fries.

4. Use a thermometer to control the heat of the oil.

5. Never leave the wok unattended over a high heat.

6. Use a wooden-handled ladle to remove cooked food from the hot oil. Drain the food well on paper towels.

COOKING TECHNIQUES

Thailand's cuisine is quick to prepare and cook – a valuable asset when time is at a premium for cooks everywhere. It is reassuring, too, to know that mastering the art of Thai cooking is not difficult and the basics can be absorbed very quickly. Although Thai dishes may seem exotic and unusual, the everyday cooking techniques used in Thai kitchens are familiar to Western cooks.

Boiling Most evening meals include a soup, in which the ingredients have been boiled together. Thais also boil water for pouring over several types of dried noodles to reconstitute them before quickly stir-frying with other ingredients. If you want to cook noodles or rice in salted water, remember to add the salt to the water after it comes to the boil because salted water takes longer to boil. A conventional heavy-based saucepan is ideal to use, but a wok works just as well.

Deep-frying Crispy, deep-fried foods are popular throughout Thailand, many of which, such as fish cakes, are served as snacks by street vendors.

The technique used by Thai cooks is identical to that used in Western kitchens, and the same guidelines for success apply. Use a vegetable oil such as sunflower, corn or peanut, with little flavour and a high smoking point, because it should be heated to about 190°C/375°F. It is a good idea to attach a deep-frying thermometer to your wok or saucepan so you make sure the oil stays at the right temperature: if it is too cool, too much oil will be absorbed and the finished dish will be greasy and unpleasant; if it is too hot, the outside will burn before the middle is cooked.

Grilling or barbecuing Thais are fond of grilling foods, especially fresh seafood, over charcoal. Meat and seafood are often marinated before they are grilled. A well-known example of a delicious, tender Thai grilled dish is satay – tender pieces of beef, pork or chicken grilled on bamboo skewers and served with a spicy peanut sauce. Originally Malaysian, there probably isn't a Thai restaurant menu in the world that doesn't feature it.

Steaming One of the most basic of all cooking techniques, steaming is well suited to the Thai cuisine because it preserves flavours and retains much of the natural moisture in ingredients. Tender steamed dishes also provide an interesting contrast in a meal to the crisper texture of ingredients that have been stir-fried or deep-fried. Steaming, which is simply cooking over boiling liquid – not in it – is an ideal way to cook delicate ingredients, such as freshly caught fish and seafood. This is because the food is not subjected to the fierce heat of frying and there isn't any oil to mask the subtle fresh seafood flavour. The steam circulating around the food creates a moist cooking environment so food remains tender because it doesn't dry out. There are health benefits from steaming food because vitamin C, present in bean-sprouts and other vegetables, is not destroyed as it is when food is boiled.

Steaming is a good technique for busy cooks without much time because several dishes can be cooked at once if you use a tiered steamer or stack several bamboo steamers on top of each other.

Thai cooks are fond of wrapping rice, meat or seafood in banana leaves with fresh herbs and spices and then steaming them to create aromatic parcels. (Large lettuce and vine leaves make acceptable alternatives.)

The most important thing to remember when steaming is to make sure the container you use is tightly sealed. This retains the heat and moisture.

Stir-frying All Thai kitchens are equipped with at least one large wok, and the list of ingredients that are suitable for stir-frying includes just about everything in the Thai daily diet – rice and noodles, fresh vegetables, meat, poultry and fish and seafood.

This fast and very easy cooking technique was developed centuries ago by the Chinese and has been adopted whole-heartedly by Thai chefs. Because stir-frying is so quick, vegetables retain their flavour and texture and meat remains tender. It is also a healthy way to cook because ingredients retain the nutrients that are destroyed by longer exposure to heat in other cooking methods.

Stir-frying involves constantly stirring small pieces of food in very little oil over a very high heat until they are cooked through. The food is cooked by both the heat of the oil and the heat of the pan. A wok is the most suitable cooking utensil for stir-frying in, but you can also use a heavy-based frying pan (skillet).

It is vital to have all your ingredients prepared before you start stir-frying.

THAI CURRIES

The Indian influence on Thai food is most evident in the popular curries, but the curries served in Thailand have their own style. This is because the Thai cooks start by pounding fresh herbs and spices, and occasionally other ingredients, together to make a wet paste, unlike in India, where curries are flavoured with blends of dry herbs and spices. Quick-cooking Thai curries are usually simmered uncovered in coconut milk and tend to contain a small proportion of solids to liquid, as the hot, spicy juices are absorbed by the rice that is the usual accompaniment. It is also an economical way to feed more people.

Green and red curry pastes are the most traditional, and every cook has a personal recipe, although there are recipes that start with orange or yellow pastes. Pastes were traditionally made by pounding ingredients in a deep, stone mortar with a heavy pestle, but as many customs are abandoned in the universal quest to save time, some modern cooks use commercially produced curry pastes, now sold in all supermarkets, and electric food processors replace the mortar and pestle.

Red curry paste, coloured by generous amounts of dried chillies, forms the basis of many beef curries, while green curry paste is usually used for chicken curries, although there are many exceptions.

SUCCESSFUL STIR-FRYING

1. Have all your ingredients prepared before you start. Thai cooking is quick, so once you start frying there won't be any time for chopping or slicing.

2. Cut ingredients to similar sizes so they all cook in the same time.

3. Heat the wok over a high heat before you add the oil; don't add any oil until smoke rises from the wok.

4. Pour the oil down the sides so they are well coated. This prevents foods from sticking.

5. Cook meat first, then add other ingredients according to how long they will take to cook, so all ingredients are tender at once.

6. Pat dry marinated fish, meat or poultry before you add it to the hot oil to prevent it from splattering.

THE CUTTING EDGE

If you ever watch a professional Thai chef chopping or slicing with a cleaver, he or she will work at lightning speed. This is because they are working with razor-sharp cutting instruments. If you intend to cook Thai food regularly, you should get into the habit of quickly sharpening your cleaver or knife each time you use it.

Using a steel is a quick and easy way to keep any blade sharp. There are several methods for using a steel but one easy technique is to use one hand to hold the steel vertically on a non-stick surface. Use your other hand to grip the handle of the cleaver or knife like a tennis racket. Hold the blade at a 20° angle to the shaft of the steel, then in a smooth, continuous movement pull the blade downwards along the length of the steel. Repeat about five times, then follow the same procedure on the other side of the blade.

COOKING UTENSILS

You don't have to buy lots of expensive equipment to cook delicious Thai meals. In fact, most Thai kitchens are modest rooms with a supply of basic, traditional utensils. Even today there are fewer gas or electric ovens and grills (broilers) than in the West, and in rural areas family meals are still cooked on open charcoal stoves. Any utensils that you don't already have can be bought in most good kitchen supply stores, large supermarkets or Oriental food stores.

Chopping boards Much Thai cooking involves chopping or slicing ingredients into small pieces, so a sturdy chopping board is a good investment. It will protect the blade on any cleaver or knife, as well as your working surface!

Cleavers and knives Traditional Thai cooks may well use only a cleaver for all their meat and vegetable preparation, while others will have a selection of knives similar to the ones found in any Western kitchen. Made in carbon or stainless steel, cleavers have a firm, trapezoid blade and can be used for chopping, slicing, mincing (grinding) and even cutting through bones. A cleaver inevitably gets lots of heavy-duty use, so buy one that has the blade forged into the handle, which means it should last longer. Large cleavers can be quite heavy; the heaviest ones are for cutting through meat bones.

If you want to use a more conventional knife, however, make sure you have a good, general-purpose kitchen knife, also called a cook's or chef's knife. The blades come in a variety of lengths, but one 20–25 cm/8–10 inches long is useful for most preparations and easy to handle. Formal or celebration meals in Thailand often feature elaborately carved fruit decorations and this is done with a small fluting knife. Smaller than most paring knives, the blade on this type of knife is curved into a half-moon shape and it has a very sharp point.

Cutting utensils made from carbon steel can be given razor-sharp edges, but they tarnish and have to be carefully washed and dried immediately after each use. Stainless-steel blades on the other hand can't be made as sharp but they don't tarnish or rust. If you are buying a new cleaver or knife, it is simply a matter of personal choice which material you select, as both make excellent knives.

Deep-frying ladle This simple strainer with a long wooden handle and a coarse wire basket at the end is used for removing deep-fried food from hot fat, or scooping ingredients out of boiling liquids. You can substitute a slotted draining spoon.

Ginger grater Many Thai recipes require the refreshing flavour of fresh ginger (ginger root) but not its texture, and this is achieved by using a grater specifically designed for ginger. The grater's surface has rows of tiny, spike-like bumps which bruise and break down the ginger's fibres to release the juice, rather than just cutting or shredding the flesh, which is what happens when a standard Western grater is used. These graters are traditionally made out of white ceramic but you can also find wooden ones. Also popular with Japanese and Chinese chefs, these are often sold in Chinese supermarkets, or specialist kitchen shops.

Pestle and mortar Most Thai homes own two of these traditional pieces of equipment for grinding spices and crushing herbs and other ingredients into pastes: a coarse stone one strong enough to withstand heavy pounding to make a finely ground mixture, ideal for preparing moist curry pastes in, and a wooden one for more gentle blending. A small food processor or coffee grinder, used exclusively for grinding herbs and spices, makes a less labour-intensive substitute.

Saucepan A large heavy-based saucepan is ideal for cooking rice, an essential component of Thai meals. Make sure that any saucepan you use for cooking rice has a tight-fitting lid. Numerous saucepans hanging from the ceiling were once a regular sight in Thai kitchens but they are now being replaced by electric rice cookers.

Steamer Inexpensive bamboo steamers that could be stacked over a pan of boiling water were once the norm in Thai kitchens, but now these are being replaced by multi-tiered aluminium or stainless-steel steamers. Stainless-steel steamers with interleaved perforated panels that fit inside saucepans are inexpensive and work well, although they only hold a limited quantity of ingredients.

Steamers are not expensive and are good investments even if you do not intend to do a lot of Thai cooking because they can be used for a lot of Western-style cooking as well. If you buy one of the ones that doesn't have a built-in saucepan on the bottom, be sure to check that it fits comfortably in or on top of your saucepans. The top must be able to close completely for it to be effective.

Wok This economical and versatile cooking utensil will become invaluable if you cook a lot of Thai food, although a large, heavy-based frying pan (skillet) is an adequate substitute. A large wok can be used for stir-frying, deep-frying, boiling and even steaming when you place a bamboo steamer inside it. Chinese food stores are a good source of inexpensive, but well-made, woks.

Like a frying pan, a wok is used directly over the heat source, but its design, with its curved sides and rounded base, distributes the heat evenly, creating a cooking surface much larger than on a similar-sized frying pan.

Woks are made in all materials, including some with non-stick surfaces. Most woks have one long handle but another useful and widely available design has two handles on the sides, which makes it easier to handle.

The two features to look for when buying a wok are a wooden handle that won't get too hot and a round burner ring, also called a wok stand. This goes over the gas flame or electric element on top of the stove and stabilizes a round-bottom wok, so it remains stable while you are cooking.

A WELL-SEASONED WOK

To prevent food sticking while it is being stir-fried, you should 'season' your wok before using it the first time, unless it has a non-stick surface, in which case, follow the manufacturer's instructions.

To season a wok, heat it over a high heat until the surface is hot, then remove it from the heat and stir in about 1 tablespoon of flavourless vegetable oil. Use a double thickness of kitchen paper (paper towels) to rub the entire surface with oil. Repeat this process twice more, then rinse the inside of the wok with water and dry it thoroughly. If it isn't dried thoroughly, rust will develop and you will have to scour it and season it again.

GRATING GINGER

Some recipes specify to grate ginger before it is cooked with other ingredients. To do this, just peel the flesh and rub it at a 45°angle up and down on the fine section of a metal grater, or use a special wooden or ceramic ginger grater.

WOK TIP

Always heat your wok before you add oil or other ingredients. This will prevent anything from sticking to it.

233

OPENING A FRESH COCONUT

Use a metal skewer to pierce the three round 'eyes' on the top of the shell, then shake out the liquid. (This is coconut water and can be added to curries and other dishes but it doesn't have much flavour.) Place the shell on a hard surface and tap it around the middle until it cracks in half. Prise the white meat away with a sharp knife and peel off the thin brown skin. Cut the meat into pieces or grate it. It can be frozen for up to two months.

MAKING FRESH COCONUT MILK

Place about 250 g/8 oz/1 cup grated coconut in a heatproof bowl and pour in 600 ml/ 1 pint/2½ cups boiling water, or enough to just cover the coconut. Leave for 1 hour. Strain through a colander lined with muslin (cheesecloth), then gather up the muslin and squeeze out as much of the thicker liquid as possible. You can also use unsweetened desiccated (shredded) coconut.

THAI INGREDIENTS

The wonderful, exotic flavours of Thai food are created by a combination of ingredients, many of which Western cooks are very familiar with, while others are not as well known. Here is a guide to the most frequently used ingredients in Thai cooking. Some of these are easily found in supermarkets, while others are only available from stores selling Asian and Oriental groceries.

Bamboo shoots These cream-coloured shoots add a crunchy texture to stir-fries. They are not sold fresh, but you will find cone-shaped whole shoots or slices in cans and occasionally dried ones, which need to be soaked in water before they are used. Once canned shoots have been opened, drain off the liquid and transfer any unused ones to a bowl of water and store in the refrigerator for up to five days, changing the water daily.

Banana leaves Thai cooks use these large green inedible leaves for wrapping around food before it is steamed or baked, and sometimes as large platters for serving food on. During the cooking process, the leaves impart a slightly aromatic flavour and sometimes a pale green colour. Do not eat these leaves.

Basil A species of basil grown in Thailand, called Holy basil or Thai basil, has a much sharper, more pungent flavour and thinner leaves than that of the sweet basil commonly grown in the West. Thai basil is not eaten raw, but instead is added to meat and fish curries while they cook. Look in specialist Oriental food stores for this; even if you can't find the fresh plant you may find seeds which are easy to cultivate. Substitute sweet basil if unavailable.

Bean sauce Sold in cans or jars, this spicy, thick sauce is made from crushed yellow or black soya beans, flour, vinegar, salt and a selection of spices. It is used to intensify the flavour of many cooked dishes, and salt usually isn't needed after this is added. You might find it labelled as 'salted black beans'. The sauce will keep almost indefinitely in its container at room temperature, unless you live in a hot, humid area, where it should be refrigerated.

Bean-sprouts Tiny, crunchy mung bean sprouts are added to salads and stir-fries. Fresh sprouts, available from supermarkets, are best eaten on the day of purchase, although they can be kept in an air-tight container in the refrigerator for several days. Canned bean sprouts are sold but they have less texture and taste.

Chilli paste Made from ground roasted chillies and oil, this is sold in small jars, and may be simply labelled 'ground chillies in oil'. The flavour is concentrated and usually very hot, so only use a small amount at a time. It will keep indefinitely in a sealed container.

Chilli sauce Thai cooks occasionally add this flavouring to other ingredients while they are cooking, but usually it is served as a side dish for dipping crispy fried or grilled (broiled) foods into. Whenever you prepare a Thai meal, be sure to put small bowls of chilli sauce on the table. Chilli sauces with varying degrees of heat are used throughout Asia, but in Thailand they tend to be slightly sweetened and have a clear, bright red appearance with small pieces of dried chillies. Numerous commercial brands are sold, and some Oriental grocers make up their own recipe. You will often find bottles of Thai chilli sauce labelled as just chicken or fish sauce.

Chillies, dried A good substitute for fresh chillies, these are generally added whole to other ingredients but sometimes a recipe will specify to halve them first. In either case, they are usually removed from a dish before it is served. Dried chillies should keep for up to a year in a cool, dark place.

Chillies, fresh More than half a dozen of the world's hottest chillies grow in Thailand, and it is the tiny but searingly hot bird's-eye chilli that produces much of the heat in Thai recipes.

Chilli peppers come in a variety of colours and shapes with varying degrees of heat, but as a general rule, the smaller a chilli is, the hotter it will be. Many of the chillies regularly used in Thai cooking are familiar to Western cooks and easily available – Anaheim, cayenne, jalapeño, New Mexican, serrano and bird's-eye chillies. If you are new to Thai cooking, use one of the milder chillies, such as the Anaheim, and then gradually replace it with one of the hotter ones. Chopped fresh hot chillies can be replaced with chilli paste

or chilli powder in recipes, but the result will be slightly different. Take care not to rub your eyes or mouth after you have prepared fresh chillies without first washing your hands.

Coconut In one form or another, coconut appears in most Thai meals, with the fresh meat used in both sweet and savoury cookery for its characteristic flavour. When you buy a coconut, make sure it feels heavy for its size and has enough liquid inside that you can hear it sloshing around when you shake the coconut. An uncracked coconut will keep for about one month at room temperature. After you crack it open, keep the flesh, well wrapped, in the refrigerator for up to five days.

Coconut milk This liquid is not the liquid found inside coconuts – that is called coconut water. Coconut milk, used to flavour meat and fish dishes, as well as desserts and drinks, is made from the white coconut flesh soaked in water or milk and then squeezed to extract all the flavour.

You can make your own coconut milk using a fresh coconut, or buy it in cans. It is also possible to buy solid bars of creamed coconut, which produce coconut milk when mixed with boiling water. Do not confuse coconut milk with coconut cream, or cream of coconut, a thick, sweet liquid used for cocktails.

Coriander (cilantro) Both the roots and leaves of this fragrant herb are used in Thai dishes. The roots are usually added during the cooking process, while the

USING CREAMED COCONUT

Bars of creamed coconut make coconut milk that is creamier and richer than when fresh coconut meat is used. Instructions will be on the package, but as a rough guide, crumble a specific weight of creamed coconut into a heatproof bowl and then stir in twice as much boiling water. For example, to make 250 ml/8 fl oz/1 cup, use 75 g/3 oz/6 tbsp creamed coconut and 175 ml/6 fl oz/¾ cup water.

TAMARIND LIQUID

The tamarind pulp sold in Asian and Oriental food stores has to be soaked in boiling liquid before it is used to give food a sharp and sour flavour. All you have to do is soak about 30 g/1 oz pulp in 300 ml/½ pint/1¼ cups boiling water for about 20 minutes. Then strain the liquid through a non-metallic sieve (strainer), pressing down on the pulp with a wooden spoon.

NOODLES

Many different varieties of noodles are used in Thai cooking, and most are interchangeable. Dried noodles need to be soaked in cold water before they are used, during which time they will double in weight. They then require only a very short cooking time, and are ideal for using in stir-fry recipes. Fresh noodles are ready to use and also only require a short cooking time. The most typical Thai noodles are:

Cellophane noodles Made from ground mung beans, these are thin, almost transparent and flavourless. They are also called bean thread noodles and often used in Thai soups and some stir-fry dishes. Always sold dry.

leaves are more often used fresh for adding flavour to cooked dishes; the stems are also ground and used to make curry pastes. Although this is a member of the parsley family and looks similar to flat-leaf parsley, the flavour is very different, and the two herbs are not interchangeable. Coriander (cilantro) will keep in water for about five days, or in the refrigerator in a plastic bag.

Curry leaves These look like bay leaves but are not as thick. They are highly aromatic when chopped, and are often included in slow-simmering dishes, such as curries, reflecting an Indian influence on Thai cuisine. Olive green in colour, curry leaves are sold fresh or dried.

Fish paste Made from fermented fish or shrimp and salt, this thick paste is used in small amounts because it is so strong. Anchovy paste makes a good substitute.

Fish sauce An essential staple throughout Thailand, this thin brown sauce with a pungent flavour is used as a seasoning during cooking and at the table, much like soy sauce is used in China and Japan. Consequently, very little salt is used in Thai cooking. Fish sauce is made by layering fish and salt in large barrels and then leaving the mixture to ferment for about four months, when the liquid is poured off. You will usually finds bottles of this labelled with its Thai name – *nam pla*.

Galangal Resembling fresh ginger root in appearance, this rhizome has pale yellow flesh and pink shoots. It is also known as

Thai ginger, or laos. The root is not used alone, but usually ground and then combined with other ingredients to make the base of red or green curry pastes, or it is added to soups and steamed vegetables. Fresh and dried galangal are sold at Asian food stores. Store the fresh root in an air-tight container in the refrigerator.

Garlic A common ingredient in the Thai kitchen, garlic is also served pickled as a side dish or thinly sliced and deep-fried as a crispy garnish. Thai garlic bulbs tend to be smaller than the ones sold in the West, so they need not be peeled before use, but peeling is necessary for Western garlic, unless it is very young and tender. Store fresh garlic in an air-tight container in the refrigerator.

Kaffir lime leaves These are dark green, glossy leaves with a lemon-lime flavour that are used as bay leaves are used in Western cooking. If you can't find any, substitute the finely pared rind of 1 lime.

Lemon grass This aromatic plant, with its distinctive slight citrus fragrance and lemon flavour, looks like a fibrous spring onion (scallion) and is frequently included in Thai soups and stews. Only the stalk is used, and it should be bashed or split along its length to release all the flavour during cooking. It is then usually discarded before the dish is served. Some Asian shops also sell dried lemon grass.

Limes Used for flavouring and garnishing, limes are an important ingredient in many Thai dishes.

Oyster sauce Despite being made from dried oysters, this thick, rich brown sauce doesn't have any hint of the flavour of oysters. Instead, it tastes salty-sweet and is usually used to flavour stir-fries. It is sold in bottles, and once opened, it should be stored in the refrigerator.

Palm sugar A thick, coarse brown sugar with a slightly caramel taste. It is sold in round cakes or in small round flat containers. Soft dark brown or demerara sugars are good alternatives.

Rice All Thai meals include rice, both the long-grain fragrant Thai rice and the shorter, glutinous 'sticky' rice, called this because its high gluten content cooks into a sticky mess. Although sticky rice is often used in desserts, it also features in main courses as stuffings or wrapped in leaves with meat and spices to make parcels that are steamed or boiled. When fragrant Thai rice is unavailable, substitute basmati or another high-quality long-grain rice; use Italian arborio rice as a substitute for sticky rice.

Rice vinegar This slightly sweet vinegar is less acidic than most Western vinegars. Cider vinegar can be used as a substitute.

Shrimp paste Similar to fish paste, but made exclusively with shrimp, this is very pungent and should be used sparingly. Cooking transforms the off-putting odour, so shrimp paste is fried or roasted before it is combined with other ingredients. It is sold as a bar of fresh paste or as a ground powder. If you have the paste, store it in the refrigerator in a tightly sealed container or its strong odour will permeate other foods.

Tamarind One of the ingredients that gives Thai cuisine its special sweet and sour taste. The pulp of the tamarind tree is compressed into a dark-brown slab which needs to be soaked in boiling water before use to remove the fibres and seeds. Asian grocery stores sell tamarind paste and tamarind juice, both ready to use. Vinegar diluted with water or water can be used as substitutes but neither the flavour nor colour are exactly the same.

Tofu Also called bean curd, this creamy coloured, mild-tasting ingredient is made from compressed soy beans. Available plain or smoked, tofu is a good source of protein and ideal for vegetarian diets. It is useful for cooks as it absorbs the flavours of other ingredients it is cooked with. Pressed tofu can be cubed for stir-frying or cooking with other ingredients, while the softer, creamier silken tofu is used in dressings or desserts. Store tofu in the refrigerator in a bowl of water for about five days, changing the water daily.

Water chestnuts Sometimes sold fresh at Asian food stores, these are more commonly available canned. They add a crunchy texture and slightly sweet taste to dishes. Store like bamboo shoots.

Wonton skins These are thin sheets of pale-coloured dough used for wrapping around sweet and savoury mixtures before they are fried or steamed. Filo or strudel pastries makes good alternatives.

Egg noodles Sold fresh in Asian markets or dry, these are made from wheat flour, eggs and water so they have a yellow appearance, and are rolled very thinly. These can be boiled or steamed.

Rice noodles Similar in taste and appearance to cellophane noodles, except that these are made with ground rice rather than mung beans. Rice ribbon noodles are long and cut to a width similar to Italian tagliatelle, while rice stick noodles are shorter. Rice vermicelli are long, thin noodles that cook almost instantly; just soak quickly and drain before adding to a stir-fry, but deep-fry without soaking.

INDEX